THE CRITICS DEBATE

General Editor: Michael Scott

The Critics Debate

General Editor Michael Scott

Published titles

Further titles are in preparation

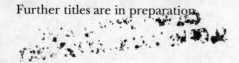

HOWARDS END

Malcolm Page

MACMILLAN

First published 1993 by
THE MACMILLAN PRESS LTD
Houndmills, Basingstoke, Hampshire RG21 2XS
and London
Companies and representatives
throughout the world

ISBN 0–333–48848–2 hardcover
ISBN 0–333–48849–0 paperback

A catalogue record for this book is available
from the British Library

Copy-edited and typeset by Cairns Craig Editorial, Edinburgh

Printed in Hong Kong

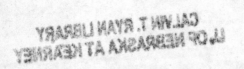

To Antony

Contents

Contents

General Editor's Preface

OVER THE last few years the practice of literary criticism has become hotly debated. Methods developed earlier in the century and before have been attacked and the word 'crisis' has been drawn upon to describe the present condition of English Studies. That such a debate is taking place is a sign of the subject discipline's health. Some would hold that the situation necessitates a radical alternative approach which naturally implies a 'crisis situation'. Others would respond that to employ such terms is to precipitate or construct a false position. The debate continues but it is not the first. 'New Criticism' acquired its title because it attempted something fresh, calling into question certain practices of the past. Yet the practices it attacked were not entirely lost or negated by the new critics. One factor became clear: English Studies is a pluralistic discipline.

What are students coming to advanced work in English for the first time to make of all this debate and controversy? They are in danger of being overwhelmed by the cross-currents of critical approaches as they take up their study of literature. The purpose of this series is to help delineate various critical approaches to specific literary texts. Its authors are from a variety of critical schools and have approached their task in a flexible manner. Their aim is to help the reader come to terms with the variety of criticism and to introduce him or her to further reading on the subject and to a fuller evaluation of a particular text by illustrating the way it has been approached in a number of contexts. In the first part of the book a critical survey is given of some of the major ways the text has been appraised. This is done sometimes in a thematic manner, sometimes according to various 'schools' or 'approaches'. In the second part the authors provide their own appraisals of the text from their stated critical standpoint, allowing the reader the knowledge of their own particular approaches from which their views may in turn be evaluated. The series therein hopes to introduce and to elucidate criticism of authors and texts being studied and to encourage participation as the critics debate.

Michael Scott

Introduction

I first read *Howards End* when I was seventeen. Like Leonard, I aspired to this cultivated life where people talked fluently of Monet and Debussy. I responded more strongly to the presenting of subtleties and nuances, unspoken undercurrents, 'the lights and shades that exist in the grayest conversation' (p. 188), and wondered if I lacked this kind of deep sensitivity.

Years later I lived near the house which was the original of Howards End, and several times leaned on the gate and thought of the characters' adventures there and about picturesque old houses in the country. Then I turned the other way and looked at the red rust of Stevenage spreading, still several fields away from the house.

When I next read the novel I was surprised to see the criticism of Culture I had missed, and also the way in which the beauty of Nature finally mattered more than all Culture. Such approaches focused on ideas more than either story or characters.

Howards End appeared in 1910. This is the year in which, as Virginia Woolf famously and provocatively observed, 'human character changed' ('Mr Bennett and Mrs Brown', 1924, p. 96). She attributed this change to a Post-Impressionist exhibition, a connection between England and Europe, one of Forster's subjects. In terms of the English novel of his time, Forster claims a place somewhere between the hugely popular H. G. Wells, Arnold Bennett and John Galsworthy and the highbrow work of the late Henry James. At this date James Joyce and D. H. Lawrence are about to introduce more experimental fictional techniques and gerater sexual explicitness. Forster is most often placed as looking back for his models, to the social comedy of Jane Austen, and to George Meredith – usually a secondhand judgement, as few nowadays read Meredith.

The Manuscripts of 'Howards End', edited by Oliver Stallybrass, were published in 1973. These reveal how carefully Forster worked over the text, correcting and rewriting many times. He often changes a neutral word to a more colourful one. He apparently saw a risk that Aunt Juley was becoming too prominent – and too amusing – and cut some of her scenes and remarks. Less significant, Leonard starts out as James and as Edward, while Helen takes a walking stick, not an umbrella, from Queen's Hall. The manuscripts also show a little self-censorship about sex. John H. Stape, however, warns that the *Manuscripts* contains numerous errors of omission and commission (1976) and Stallybrass subsequently defended his work (1976). One alteration in the Abinger edition comes at the end of Chapter 2, when Aunt Juley catches the train to Hilton: 'Mrs Munt secured a comfortable seat, facing the engine, but not too near it' (27). The American Signet Classic still has instead the longer statement: 'Mrs Munt, though she took a second-class ticket, was put by the guard into a first (only two seconds on the train, one smoking and the other babies – one cannot be expected to travel with babies)' (New York, 1986, p. 11). The present, presumably correct, form, could hardly be more banal, which is needed to contrast with the elevated start of the paragraph, that 'the station of King's Cross had always suggested infinity' to Margaret.

Two thousand five hundred copies were originally printed: Forster's contract with his publisher, Edward Arnold, was more generous than for his previous novels. Yet he needed sales of at least five thousand copies to have an adequate income. Only in recent years have the issues of negotiations between author and publisher, sales' figures and earnings taken their rightful place as an essential part of the study of a text. For Forster, Philip Gardner supplies the key facts in his introduction to *E. M. Forster: The Critical Heritage* (1973). Peter Keating puts Forster's sales and earnings in the context of the other leading novelists of his time in Chapter 7 of his *The Haunted Study* (1989). N. N. Feltes makes the novel a key early example of 'the book as commodity' in his *Modes of Production of Victorian Novels* (1986).

This study arises almost entirely from the text of *Howards End* and the dozens who have written about it. I have drawn on three non-fiction texts by Forster for insights, the essay collections, *Abinger Harvest* and *Two Cheers for Democracy*, and his thoughts on the genre in lectures entitled – in a typically disarming way – *Aspects of the Novel*. I also refer to interviews he gave, and to the other four novels published in his lifetime. Otherwise, a sense of the evolution of the novel just before and after the year of *Howards End*, and also of the social and political history of Britain at the time is implicit.

Howards End has earned additional attention through the stage, television and radio, as often in the twentieth century. Lance Sieveking adapted the book for BBC radio in 13 parts in 1964, and Jeffrey Segal into just four parts in 1985: Joanne Pearce played Margaret, Miranda Richardson Helen and Gwen Watford Mrs Wilcox in the latter. A stage version, adapted by Sieveking and Richard Cottrell, appeared in the West End in London in February 1967. This time Gwen Watford played Margaret with Gemma Jones as Helen. Mrs Wilcox and Evie were left out; David Benedictus summed up in *Plays and Players*: 'It is hard to think of any novelist whose works are done a greater injustice by this watering down, and simmering up, and luke-warm serving' (May 1967). Pauline Macaulay dramatised it for a glossy BBC television version, produced by Cedric Messina, in April 1970, with Glenda Jackson as Margaret and Rachel Kempson as Mrs Wilcox. Quite how much was left out – quite apart from the all-important narratorial voice – is revealed in the review in *The Times*: 'We were treated to an ever changing vista of gracious living. It was all greenery, sunshine, tea cups and the gleam of beautiful cars' (Leonard Buckley, 20 April 1970, p. 13). *Beautiful cars!* What about London? What about Leonard? Though *Howards End* may be impossible to realise in any other medium, a film version was released in 1992, scripted by Ruth Prawer Jhabvala and directed by James Ivory, with Emma Thompson as Margaret, Helena Bonham Carter as Helen, Vanessa Redgrave as Mrs Wilcox and Anthony Hopkins as Henry Wilcox.

Students of Forster are enormously helped by two substantial American annotated bibliographies, the first by Frederick P. W. McDowell (1976) and a successor compiled by Claude J. Summers (1991). Summers' book goes up to August 1990 and mostly contains material published since McDowell finished his work in 1973. Summers lists 88 articles and chapters of books about *Howards End*.

Literary studies have, of course, been transformed in recent years by the rise of critical theory, so that much contemporary writing is peppered with terms like deconstruction and structuralism. While the bulk of criticism of Forster appears after 1960, nevertheless it remains true, as Alan Wilde wrote in 1985: 'Almost all commentary on Forster exists within a relatively familiar and traditional realm of critical discourse' ('Introduction', 1985, p. 1).

In keeping with the format of this series, Part 1 engages with some of the issues raised in the great debate of For or Against this novel. Part 2 responds to George H. Thomson, who concluded: 'If one were to ask what *Howards End* is about, the answers would probably be as varied as if one were to ask what the Fifth Symphony is about' (1967, p. 172).

This short study is not addressed to one hundred Forster specialists, nor to ten thousand critical theorists. It is addressed to those who have just read the novel and are intrigued enough to want to try to understand it more fully.

Part 1
Survey

1   The Reputation of Forster and of *Howards End*

The last novel published in Forster's lifetime, *A Passage to India*, appeared in 1924. Forster's reputation since then appears to have slumped until 1943; admiration predominated until his death in 1970; a second slump lasted until the mid-1980s; then, recently, a revival.

Frederick P. W. McDowell refers to Forster's 'obscurity' in the thirties (1982, p. 311). Though Rose Macaulay had written the first book about Forster in 1938, it was Lionel Trilling's influential *E. M. Forster*, published in the United States in 1943 and in Britain the following year, that revived his reputation. There was also the example of Forster himself, the wise old man at King's College, Cambridge, writing civilised essays and committed to such causes as civil liberties.

After Forster's death, the quality of his work is again questioned. Judith Scherer Herz observes: 'Forster's reputation has been sliding, no doubt about it, ever since his death and posthumous publication of *Maurice* and *The Life to Come*, and sliding more rapidly since P. N. Furbank's biography appeared [in 1977–78]' (1984, p. 246). Michael Bell noted in 1980: 'Forster has more slowly become the object of negative revaluation' (p. 77). Alan Wilde in 1985 asks: 'Has Forster in fact, despite the continued outpouring of books and essays devoted to him, receded from readers in general? And is his reputation less secure than it once was?' ('Introduction', p. 4).

In the second half of the eighties, interest in Forster revives, and admiration grows. A major cause may be the success of the films of *A Passage to India* (though most of the subtleties, and the ideas, of the novel were lost) and *A Room with a View*, and the more modest success of *Maurice*: a film of *Where Angels Fear to Tread* followed.

Claude Summers in 1991 is able to refer in passing to the preceding 15 years as 'a crucial period in which Forster's reputation both reached its nadir and began impressive recovery' (p. x).

The reputation of *Howards End* is of course related. Trilling was emphatic, pronouncing it 'undoubtedly Forster's masterpiece' (1943, p. 99). Trilling changed his mind, according to Stallybrass's 'Introduction' to *Howards End* (p. 16). David Shusterman wrote in 1965: 'I should judge that at least half of the critics who have written on Forster – perhaps more, since Trilling's influence has been considerable – have thought that it is his masterpiece' (p. 143). Thereafter the popular, if somewhat pointless, game of which novel was best was won instead by *A Passage to India* and by 1973 a *Times Literary Supplement* reviewer spoke of the 'inflated reputation' of *Howards End* ('Patriarch of the Liberal Imagination', 26 October 1973, p. 1316). McDowell noted in 1982 that in recent years 'critics have been less attentive to *Howards End* than to *A Passage to India*' (p. 325). The preference for *A Passage to India* continues, because of attention to weighty questions of colonialism and its consequences, and the ambitious contrasting of Hinduism, Mohammedanism and 'poor little talkative Christianity'.

Collecting hostile evaluations of *Howards End* is easy. John Batchelor qualifies his views: 'It seems to me an honourable failure, a noble attempt to do far too much and be too many kinds of writer' (1982, p. 226). Harry Blamires is harsher: 'Those for whom Forster's message catches fire claim it as a masterpiece, the last word in condemnation of people whose life is determined by catchwords and who sin against passion and truth. But the artifices of the assault upon artifice have always offended others' (1982, p. 45). An anonymous writer in the *Times Literary Supplement* was stronger, finding it 'Heavy with the liberal sentimentality that sometimes passed for thought in Forster, and seriously flawed by his inability to deal with the central issue of men, women and sex' ('All that the scholar could want', 18 January 1974, p. 43). While Angus Wilson stated bluntly that he felt 'increasingly certain that taken as a whole, *Howards End* is a bad book' ('Books versus Biceps', *The Observer*, 7 October 1972, p. 39).

P. J. M. Scott can speak for the other side: this is 'one of the major masterpieces of Narrative art' and 'a major work on anybody's scale' (1984, pp. 113, 130). Laurence Brander describes the work as 'part of the evolving social consciousness of the English people' (1968,

p. 162). John Rosselli, more precisely, found it 'one of the last great statements about England as a whole civilisation' (*The Guardian*, June 1970).

Mary Gibson concludes that '*Howards End* is a novel critics love to hate. More even than *A Passage to India*, *Howards End* unsettles its readers as it challenges both aesthetic and political premises. The usual tone of response to the novel is mingled delight and disappointment, delight in Forster's ironies and disappointment at his unhappy happy ending' (1985, p. 106).

2 Are There Flaws of Plot and Characterisation?

Three of the major characters have been faulted from time to time – Henry, Margaret and, especially, Leonard. So have the lesser figure of Jacky and a throwaway line about Dolly. Two key events, the marriage of Henry and Margaret and Leonard and Helen's night together, have also frequently been found implausible. These will be examined in turn.

i   Henry Wilcox
Henry is the novel's chief flaw. A caricature of a businessman, he is stiff, easily muddled, utterly imperceptive about himself and others, and without a grain of redeeming wit and humour. [He] possesses not a single attribute that a woman like Margaret could conceivably love.   (John Sayre Martin, 1976, pp. 114–15, 122)

Many critics have been so mesmerized by his moral obtuseness that they have failed to recognise either his spiritual acuteness or his charm, and have underrated his commonsense and clear-sightedness. (R. N. Parkinson, London, 1979, p. 64)

Henry is of course a typical businessman, a relative of Boss Mangan in Shaw's *Heartbreak House* and of Galsworthy's *Man of Property*. Sometimes he fulfils this in his best *Daily Telegraph* editorial manner: 'The poor are poor, and one's sorry for them, but there it is. As civilization moves forward, the shoe is bound to pinch in places, and it's absurd to pretend that anyone is responsible personally . . . By all means subscribe to charities – subscribe to them largely – but don't get carried away by absurd schemes of Social Reform' (p. 192). He is contemptuous of Parliament, believing (or knowing) 'the more important ropes of life lay elsewhere' (p. 165). He is differentiated from other businessmen, such as his son Charles, by a greater gift for making money. He personifies the outer life of telegrams and anger.

Henry is placed as a 'type': 'Some day – in the millenium – there may be no need for his type' (p. 165). In fact, as with Leonard, initially a 'type' (pp. 123, 152) to both Margaret and Henry, readers are to learn that Henry is more than a type. He is a man ready to marry the unusual Ruth Howard. Henry 'preserved a gift that [Margaret] supposed herself to have already lost – not youth's creative power, but its self-confidence and optimism' (p. 165). This is shown, notably in his commanding way of buying Oniton and planning to build the marital home at Midhurst. Henry recognizes Mrs Wilcox's spiritual values, goodness, tenderness, innocence (p. 99), if in a condescending way. He is 'inherently hospitable' (p. 227), like the Schlegels. He has 'tact of a sort – the sort that is as useful as the genuine' (p. 218). He is ready to help Leonard in a 'slapdash' way (p. 229), getting on with what's needed in a practical way contrasting with 'Helen and her friends ... discussing the ethics of salvation' (p. 229). He shows brisk commonsense in preventing Charles from pursuing a feud with the chauffeur (p. 110). Near the end, this enthusiastic motorist is 'very fond of walking' and just after he lays a hand on Charles's sleeve (p. 319), a new gesture for him – Margaret is really altering him!

Henry's final total collapse, however, reveals suppressed feelings. Henry is not only the businessman but an example of the 'undeveloped heart' which Forster found in English men, especially when educated at public schools. While the Wilcoxes represent the undeveloped heart (and surely Charles and Paul would be sent to public schools), the actual heart of which we learn in the novel is Leonard's, who dies of heart disease, accelerated by Charles's blows.

ii   Margaret Schlegel
How [Margaret] does preach at us, how she bosses, what a passionless prig she now appears, in other words, how unsympathetic!   (Walter Allen, 1955, p. 408)

Margaret is the 'most striking and completely realised character' in all Forster's work.   (K. W. Gransden, 1962, p. 54)

This contrast can be continued. McDowell: 'At points, she is a bit too assured of her values (the Wilcoxes "were deficient where she excelled") or too complacent about her own existence ("culture had worked in her own case"); she may strike us as a bit overbearing towards the Wilcoxes; and she is sometimes embarrassingly direct in proclaiming her ideas' (1969, p. 94). Glen Cavaliero defends her: 'If Margaret is in some danger of seeming a prig, she is saved from this not only by the actual outcome of events, and the tragic realisation of her mistakes, but by lesser touches, such as the way we see her through other people's eyes – Leonard's, for instance (the "toothy one"), or those of Charles and Dolly' (1979, p. 123).

Understanding Margaret requires understanding two very different sides. She is formidably intellectual, awesomely articulate, confidently self-knowing. At leisure, she has evolved a fuller and more imaginative Philosophy of Life when we first meet her than most people ever do. Yet also she trusts her instincts; 'Margaret was impulsive. She did swing rapidly from one decision to another' (p. 26). Her instincts are often wrong: allowing Aunt Juley to undertake the mission to Howards End (p. 26); writing the better-we-not-meet letter to Mrs Wilcox (p. 77); refusing Mrs Wilcox's sudden invitation to Howards End (p. 93).

Crucially, Margaret changes through the book; almost, this is The Education of Margaret. She grows, changes, learns, matures. She has 'innumerable false starts' (p. 208). She admits, endearingly: 'Of course, I have everything to learn – absolutely everything – just as much as Helen. Life's very difficult and full of surprises. At all events, I've got as far as that' (p. 83). Especially she changes in the second half, after her engagement to Henry. She is turning loyally into a Wilcox when she tells Miss Avery that Wilcoxes 'keep England going' (p. 268). She is disconcertingly dutiful as a wife: Henry 'had only to call, and she clapped the book up and was ready to do what he wished' (p. 255). A Moment of Truth follows when Henry will not connect (p. 300) and Margaret, forced to choose, selects sister over husband. Then the healing, under the influence of Howards End, can begin, and she can truly become Mrs Wilcox, closely resembling the first Mrs Wilcox. Look for change in Margaret – however decisive many of her statements and thoughts in the early

part are – and the difficulties go away, though – like goblins – they
might return.

iii   *The Marriage of Henry and Margaret*

It is difficult to accept the verisimilitude of the marriage on a
literal level, it being hard to believe Margaret could marry a
man who is so obviously lacking in all the qualities she values
most.   (H. M. Daleski, 1985, p. 121)

Moved by pity and unworthiness, anxious both to appreciate and
to improve Henry (and indeed all Wilcoxes), still perhaps overly
idealistic, surely too eager to see other points of view than her
own and to do justice to them, influenced in the end by her
desire for order and for proportion and by her feeling that
these are to be achieved only by doing some violence to her
own impulses and wishes, Margaret is, after all, genuinely in
love.   (Alan Wilde, 1964, p. 114)

Such contrasting views can be continued. F. R. Leavis was emphatic
and laconic: 'Nothing in the exhibition of Margaret's or Henry
Wilcox's character makes the marriage credible or acceptable'
(1952, p. 269). Opposing, Claude J. Summers: 'Forster's depiction
of their courtship is entirely believable. Indeed, the subtlety with
which he develops their attraction for each other is a major
achievement of the novel. Margaret's attraction for Henry is a
response to his masculinity and decisiveness, his optimism and
self-confidence. Not insignificantly, she is also attracted to him
sexually' (1983, p. 127).

Criticism of the plausibility of the marriage may result from
seeing it first as a schematic necessity (connecting) and then
looking for reasons for scepticism, rather than from any basic
improbability.

Few have much difficulty with Henry's wish to marry Margaret.
He has had thirty years with a nurturing wife, content to meet all his
needs, succeeded by daughter Evie, now engaged and soon to leave
him. Henry can also half-detect in Margaret qualities he admired
in his first wife.

Margaret responds to a number of Henry's qualities, some of
which are more in the eye of the beholder than in Henry. She
'like[s] him very much' (p. 114) when he sends Mrs Wilcox's

silver vinaigrette (which now needs glossing as an ornamental bottle for smelling salts). Like much of her view of Henry, this is based on misunderstanding his motive. John Colmer stresses that Henry 'embodies the importance of work, not normally a sufficient reason for deciding to marry a man, certainly, but for Margaret a vital one. She comes to recognize that the world of culture would not exist without the Wilcoxes' hard work' (1975, p. 102). She finds he has 'charm' (p. 138), that he prefers her to her prettier sister (p. 160) and that for her he is 'a real man' (p. 176). She respects him: 'It amazed her that a man of any standing should take her seriously' (p. 169) – though he may not truly take her seriously. He is a 'stimulus, [banishing] morbidity' (p. 165); outwardly, he is 'cheerful, reliable and brave' (p. 188); to her he has a 'sensible and generous brain' (p. 209).

Aged 31, she is vulnerable at this time: 'Depressed at her isolation, she saw not only houses and furniture but the vessel of life itself slipping past her, with people like Evie and Mr Cahill on board' (p. 155). On the day of the proposal she feels 'old-maidish' (p. 163). Jacky had sung, 'Boys, I'm on the shelf' (p. 64) and Margaret and her world are conventional enough for her to be uneasy about accepting spinsterhood. She confesses: 'In my absurd way, I'm lonely too' (p. 164). The proposal comes when she is about to be homeless, without Wickham Place which 'had helped to balance' her life (p. 154). Finding herself incompetent at dealing with the approaching crisis of homelessness, Henry's practicality turns him, in her eyes, into a Knight in Shining Armour.

Further, she is ready to take risks, to make leaps of faith: this facet of Margaret is easily missed. But she claims 'I hope to risk things all my life' (p. 71) and 'hoped that for the future she would be less cautious' (p. 115). She also has the common delusion, sung in *Guys and Dolls*, that she can 'Marry the man today / And change his ways tomorrow'. 'Margaret hoped to help him. It did not seem so difficult. She need trouble him with no gift of her own. She would only point out the salvation that was latent in his own soul, and in the soul of every man. Only connect!' (p. 188). This is Margaret's naïveté, that she can hope to alter him, particularly as he is much older. Further, she is convinced that she can keep vital parts of herself apart from the marriage: 'I don't intend him, or any man or any woman, to be all my life – good heavens, no!' The narrator adds that 'she was to keep her independence more than do most women as yet' (p. 177).

Margaret first tells Helen that she does not love Henry (p. 176). Somehow she wills herself into love in the following months, though the novel has very few hints about this process. She is markedly calculating when she reflects that 'some day she would use her love to make him a better man' (p. 240).

Lastly, perhaps Margaret's self-deception in marrying Henry is a criticism of the limitations of Margaret before the painful education which comes to her in her marriage.

iv Leonard Bast

> The unreality of Bast, the principal instrument, is the defect of the novel.   (William York Tindall, 1956, p. 95)

> Leonard 'becomes, against almost impossible odds, a plausible human being'.   (F. J. Hoffman, 1964, p. 83)

Criticism of the characterisation of Leonard often springs from the knowledge that Forster had little firsthand knowledge of the world of lower middle class clerks, as he readily admitted in an interview in 1952. Asked: 'Have you ever described any type of situation of which which you have had no personal knowledge?', Forster replied: 'The home-life of Leonard and Jacky in *Howards End*. I knew nothing about that. I believe I brought it off' (Cowley, 1957, p. 28). John Colmer is completely convinced: 'There is no mistaking [Forster's] acute insight into the lives of those perched on the edge of the abyss, his deep compassion for them, and his extraordinary skill in evoking their predicament' (1975, p. 103). Forster in fact must have met men like Leonard in his teaching at the Working Men's College in Great Ormond Street in Bloomsbury, though he may never have observed their home-life. D. H. Lawrence, who created a fuller portrait of a sensitive working-class youth in Paul Morel in *Sons and Lovers* at this time, admired the portrait of Leonard. Forster told Angus Wilson: 'Lawrence could be very trying. He spent one whole afternoon condemning my work. At last I asked him if there was anything good in it. "Yes", he said, "Leonard Bast. That was courageous"' ('A Conversation with E. M. Forster', *Encounter*, 9, November 1957, p. 54).

Nevertheless, faulting the portrait of Leonard goes back to the earliest criticisms, the *Saturday Review* writer doubting whether Forster 'knows the Leonard Basts of this world' (quoted Gardner, 'Introduction', 1973, p. 13). Pat Hoy, though, finds that Leonard 'remains compelling because deep down within him there is something fine and genuine' (1985, p. 226).

Critics have struggled to place Leonard precisely within the subtleties of the British class system: 'Forster is not quite sure how to place Bast's social group. Are they really members of the middle class who, although a little poorer and less polished, one should accept? Or are they interlopers from the working class, bringing with them into the middle-class world all kinds of excesses and problems? . . . Bast is accepted into the middle class only on sufferance. He is not their equal and he has no innate right to gentility' (Mary Eagleton and David Pierce, pp. 97–8). Leonard is in fact lower middle class, his top-hat confirming this, much as tie and suit might nowadays. He can afford two shillings for a ticket for a symphony concert, even if he has to think twice about buying a programme, and economises the same day by not buying a Sunday newspaper and by walking home. Rather surprisingly, his excessive efforts at courtesy to a woman irritate Margaret because 'his class was near enough to her own for its manners to vex her' (p. 50).

Leonard starts out as half-comic and half-pathetic. He aspires to culture: 'He felt that he was being done good to, and that if he kept on with Ruskin, and the Queen's Hall concerts, and some pictures by Watts, he would one day push his head out of the gray waters and see the universe' (p. 62). (His taste in pictures appears less developed than in music and literature). Leonard actually plays the piano, jingling out Grieg badly (p. 66). This puts him ahead of the Schlegels, mere consumers of culture. Wickham Place has a piano but a Miss Quested (named only once) is the only one to use it, and then it is to play a work by the forgotten MacDowell (p. 88) – which casts some doubt on the musical discrimination of the Schlegels. Leonard is disadvantaged: little money, little education, little leisure. Unfortunately he never found his way to a class of the Workers' Educational Association, where he might have met others like himself.

Leonard grows in stature when he tells of his effort to discover the earth by walking all night in Surrey – showing individuality, enterprise and sincerity. Asked by Helen 'Was the dawn wonderful?'

he replies 'No . . . The dawn was only gray' (p. 126). When he leaves the Schlegels' house and walks down Regent Street, he is made comic again by putting on his hat: 'It was too big; his head disappeared like a pudding into a basin, the ears bending outwards at the touch of the curly brim.' The picture is amusing, then Forster adds: 'Thus equipped, he escaped criticism' (p. 131). The fault is not Leonard's, but that of a rigid society requiring hat-wearing as a sign of respectability.

Knowing Leonard also exposes both Margaret and Henry. Henry remarks glibly: 'I know the type' (p. 152). Margaret at first labels him in the same way, claiming almost arrogantly 'She knew this type very well' (p. 123). But after conversation with Leonard she is flexible and learns 'he isn't a type' (p. 152).

Later Leonard is victim: changing jobs when the well-meaning Schlegels pass on Henry's advice, then losing the one job he can do and sinking into the abyss he fears. Times are bad, as Henry 'knew by his own office – seldom a vacant post, and hundreds of applicants for it; at present no vacant post' (p. 141). Despite this, Henry is willing to try to find work for Leonard when Margaret asks him (p. 228) – until Jacky sees Henry and spoils this plan.

Forster may condescend to Leonard when he presumes that he would have been happier and better had his farmworker ancestors not brought him to the city, removing him from the Life of the Body: 'Margaret, noting the spine that might have been straight, and the chest that might have broadened, wondered whether it paid to give up the glory of the animal for a tailcoat and a couple of ideas' (p. 122). Leonard is wrong when he sees grandparents who were agricultural labourers as 'a secret than he had held shameful up to now' (p. 234).

Leonard's aspirations to culture appear doomed. Yet in *A Room with a View* another lower middle class clerk, George Emerson, is permitted to marry Lucy, the pretty young middle class girl. The only difference seems to be that George can fully appreciate Culture, because of a broadminded educated father and the chance to travel to Florence.

Forster's panorama leaves out the mass of the working class, whether employed manually or out of work. He boldly concedes this, drawing his reader in to the exclusion: 'We are not concerned with the very poor. They are unthinkable, and only to be approached by the statistician or the poet' (p. 58). This line so disgusted and horrified the heroine of Willy Russell's play, *Educating Rita*, that she abandoned reading the book. Statisticians were studying the poor: Charles Booth's massive *Life and Labour of the People in London* appeared 1889–1903 and Seebohm Rowntree's thorough survey of *Poverty* in York was published in 1901. The reference to the 'poet' calls for pause: have poets a vision no novelist can have? The very poor are already in what Forster several times calls 'the abyss'. H. G. Wells began this with a short story, 'In the Abyss', records Anne Wright (1984, p. 49) and C. F. G. Masterman's *From the Abyss* (1902), Jack London's *People of the Abyss* (1903) and Mary Higgs' *Glimpses into the Abyss* (1906) follow. Peter Keating explains the image: 'The gap between the classes is now "deep" and terrifying, a matter of delicate balance and subtle gradation, of possibly climbing up or clinging on or falling down' (1976, p. 21). Robert Tressell's account of the struggles of house-painters in Hastings, *The Ragged-Trousered Philanthropists*, posthumously published abridged in 1914, is the one accessible and informed novel of life in the abyss at this date.

Anne Wright engages with 'We are not concerned with the very poor': 'This is not, it seems to me, "innocent" narration. If "We" are not "concerned", we ought to be, and, if the abyss can indeed be *reached* only by statistics or poetry, the issue of how it is to be "approached" is of continuing concern to the novel. Both "approached" and "unthinkable" imply a genteel distaste. This is, surely, not an unthinking elitism, although it is certainly a coping mechanism. Forster adroitly *permits* his novel its delimitation, by simultaneously *admitting* the inadequacy. This first paragraph delimits the novel with subtle irony and measured self-criticism' (1984, pp. 52–3).

Forster was writing when the reforming Liberal government of Herbert Asquith, urged by David Lloyd George as Chancellor, was about to make a substantial difference to the lives of the masses with such innovations as Labour Exchanges, old age pensions and National Health Insurance. These were the forerunners of the Welfare State created by Attlee's Labour government in 1945–51.

Workers play very minor parts in *Howards End*: the bearded porter – criticised, then tipped, by Charles – who looks 'with admiration' at him (p. 32); the draper's assistant who runs to Charles's car with a roll of oilcloth (p. 33); the housemaids unwilling to work at the Schlegel house because of the 'numerous stairs' (p. 74); the

servants at Howards End who must not overhear Wilcox discussions
(p. 105); the boot man taken on by the Schlegels because he
is unemployed, who does his work badly (p. 140); the servants
who turn to saturnalia after the wedding at Oniton (p. 239); the
Schlegels' parlourmaid who gives information to Leonard (p. 312)
and the Wilcox's chauffeurs. All these have only walk-on parts, like
the butlers of *Major Barbara* and *The Importance of Being Earnest.*

v Jacky

> With Jacky, Forster is quite out of control: she is a figure
> of burlesque, and thrown about the novel like a rag doll,
> anatomised and rejected in a way quite out of keeping with
> the book's general intentions and philosophy.   (Glen Cavaliero,
> 1979, p. 117)

> The grotesque, Dickensian rendering distinguishes Jacky from
> the other characters, but the manner is appropriate to her
> role. She will blunder – painfully solid, an embarrassing
> encumbrance – through the novel. (Anne Wright, 1984,
> pp. 53–4)

Jacky is the most condemned of all the novel's characters. Peter
Widdowson finds her 'one of the few really wooden caricatures
in all of Forster's fiction' (1977, p. 91) and P. N. Furbank writes
that the novel 'has one glaring fault, the treatment of Leonard's
wife Jacky. Here I do think one runs up against grave limitations
in Forster. He truly couldn't imagine a Jacky, and here charity failed
him as well as imagination' (1974, p. 153). Even Colmer can only
half-justify Jacky by pointing to the resemblance to Dolly, Forster
linking them by the broken photographs of Chapters 7 and 8: 'Both
are silly coarse women; class is largely irrelevant' (1975, p. 96).
    We are indeed first introduced to Jacky by way of the image
of her in the photograph, which she calls her 'likeness' (p. 66),
though it has ceased to be. The Jacky of the present is prematurely
ageing and massive. Young and rather pretty, with her cute name
and seductively open mouth, she was a novelty. Smashing the
photograph frame shows she has become useless. She is dehumanised when she walks in: '"What ho!" said Leonard, greeting the
apparition with much spirit, and helping *it* off with *its* boa' (p. 63).
She is dehumanised again at Oniton, where her face gleams 'in

the twilight like a puff-ball' (p. 229). Her meal is artificial, squares dissolved in water for soup and jelly.

Jacky remains distanced, with little direct action or conversation. Helen re-tells Jacky's gutsy visit to Wickham Place in search of her wayward husband. Were we supposed to laugh along with Helen as she poked fun at Jacky's accent, her costume and her 'notty, notty' husband? 'She was incompetent! She had a face like a silkworm' (p. 121). Or are we intended to feel uncomfortable, asking ourselves whether anyone has the right to treat another human as a nonentity, a mere figure of fun? The characters, not Forster himself, may be displaying rudeness and mockery towards Jacky.

Leonard at times wants revenge on her: may he in fact have married her so that he need never risk failure on his merits with her beside him, holding him back from even trying? Leonard likes having Margaret's card with which to taunt Jacky. He would not speak to her before going for his all-night walk. Leonard is the immature one when he retorts to her: 'I know where you've been, but you don't know where I've been' (p. 130). Forster observes how unkind people are to the Jackys of the world. Mentions of Jacky come with insults. '"There's Mrs Lanoline, too," Helen yawned. "So dull"' (p. 136). 'His wife is an old bore' (p. 151). Jacky's humanity is totally disregarded when Helen says 'the card [did] see the wife' (p. 136), with card as subject and Jacky as object.

Gradually other characters are allowed to show a little sympathy for Jacky. Helen is genuinely concerned about her health when she finds them. When Margaret greets Leonard at Evie's wedding, Helen notes the bad manners and puts in 'There is Mrs Bast, too' (p. 224). Leonard, descending into the abyss, becomes more tender-hearted towards her (p. 310).

When Jacky is described as 'bestially stupid' (p. 224) the point may be that society in general believes her type must be very stupid and, as Leonard says, are more bother than they are worth (p. 225). Then, too, 'Poor Jacky! She was not a bad sort' (p. 130) and 'There was no malice in Jacky' (p. 229).

Jacky is working class, while Leonard clings to the lower middle class. She is untypical of women of her class in having been to Cyprus, in having an affair with a wealthy man, in being much older than her husband, in living with a man she is not married to, and in apparently not working. 'She never had been a great talker' (p. 64), while both Margaret and Helen have to learn to talk less.

She is 'fond of flowers' (p. 310) and 'among flowers' at the Oniton wedding reception (p. 224). Flowers are conventionally good in the book: Margaret and Aunt Juley arrange flowers together in Chapter 7; Margaret picks narcissi after Leonard's death (p. 321); Mrs Wilcox watches poppies come out (p. 20) and smells a rose after the Charles/Aunt Juley tragicomedy (p. 37); Helen has a bunch of wild flowers and grass at the end (p. 328). Jacky's 'One topic of conversation "You do love me"' (p. 64) may be pathetic, but for Forster Love is 'the Beloved Republic', which alone deserves three cheers ('What I Believe', *Two Cheers for Democracy*, 1965, p. 78).

Jacky may be a flat character (as well as a minor one) in a novel of rounded ones ('You do love me?' is her equivalent of 'I will never desert Mr Micawber'). She could have a place in other pictures of London working-class life of the time, such as Arthur Morrison's *Children of the Jago* (1896), Somerset Maugham's *Liza of Lambeth* (1897) or the West Ham Salvation Army shelter in winter in Bernard Shaw's *Major Barbara* (1905). She can, for that matter, be pictured, glass in hand, singing in a pub on Saturday night in the Mile End Road.

vi   Leonard and Helen Sleeping Together

I can never be perfectly certain whether Helen was got with child by Leonard Bast or by his fatal forgotten umbrella. All things considered, I think it must have been the umbrella.   (Katherine Mansfield, 1954, p. 121)

Helen's susceptibility to opposites – an aspect of the 'only connect' theme – provides the necessary psychological link between her brief love for Paul Wilcox and her even briefer affair with Leonard, and nearly makes both credible.   (John Colmer, 1975, p. 89)

Attacks on what was probably Helen's seduction of Leonard (since this is easier to envisage than Leonard's taking the initiative) go back to the earliest reviews, where implausibility is charged along with the picturing of immorality (see Philip Gardner, 'Introduction', 1973, p. 13). C. B. Cox thinks that 'Helen's affair with Bast remains quite incredible' (1963, pp. 78–9) and Cedric Watts that Leonard 'has fathered Helen's child in an act of copulation which, in terms of characterisation, seems wildly implausible' (1990,

p. 159). Forster himself implies some doubt: 'I did it like that out of a wish to have surprises. It has to be a surprise for Margaret, and this was best done by making it a surprise for the reader too. Too much may have been sacrificed to this' (Cowley, 1957, p. 29).

Some external factors have made critics thoroughly scrutinise this encounter. First, the novel schematically requires a connection, resulting in a child, between Schlegel and Bast (this allegorical need similarly has made critics question the marriage of Schlegel and Wilcox: see iii, above). Second, critics know Forster's own lack of heterosexual experience. And third, present-day readers expect sexual explicitness. Yet all earlier writers are self-censored; Forster's treatment is not very different from that of his contemporaries: Henry James, Arnold Bennett, John Galsworthy, Joseph Conrad. Just after the publication of *Howards End* Lawrence pushed to extend the boundaries of precisely what could be set in print, through *Sons and Lovers*, *The Rainbow*, initially successfully prosecuted, and *Lady Chatterley's Lover*, banned for over 30 years.

Helen is characterised as impulsive, lacking proportion. Especially, she 'was rather apt to entice people, and, in enticing them, to be herself enticed' (p. 44). When Leonard reappears in her life, two years after the concert at the Queen's Hall, she baits him: 'Helen didn't see why he should get off. She had the cruelty of youth' (p. 124). Late the same evening Henry tells her that Leonard's insurance company will go bankrupt, so that she plans first to write to him and then to invite him to tea (p. 143). When Leonard walks out of the tea party, Helen goes after him, and is alone with him offstage for a time, then re-enters pronouncing: 'Such a muddle of a man, and yet so worth pulling through. I like him extraordinarily' (p. 153). Next, much later, comes Helen's rescue of the penniless Basts, the wild dash to Oniton to confront Henry, and the revelation that ten years before Jacky was Henry's mistress.

Helen and Leonard converse late at night in the empty coffee-room of the George hotel in Oniton, Jacky having gone to bed. Helen disconcertingly shifts their talk from abstractions about Nietzsche to Jacky, to male-female relations. This is probably her usual manner, though it may be her special kind of sympathy – or even mischievousness. Then comes Margaret's curt notes, not only refusing Leonard a job but stating 'The Basts are not at all the type we should trouble about' (p. 239). (Margaret first saw

Leonard as a type, then said he was not (pp. 123, 152): now, at her most Wilcoxian, she reverts to labelling him – and Jacky – as a type). Directly after both have read Margaret's notes, the river murmurs and Forster lowers the curtain, leaving the rest to our prurient, or limited, imaginations.

Helen is full of guilt at the way her class has treated Leonard, and the way Henry treated Jacky. She is alienated from her sister by the offhand, unsympathetic tone of the notes. On this day she is 'dominated by [a] tense, wounding excitement' (p. 222). Leonard symbolises the exploited, oppressed poor for her. She can give him only one thing, herself. From pity and guilt, Helen takes Leonard in her arms, nature takes its course, and 'she loved him absolutely, perhaps for half an hour' (p. 308).

A little explanation comes eight months later, when Margaret and Helen stand by moonlight under the wych elm: 'Leonard seemed not a man, but a cause. Perhaps it was Helen's way of falling in love . . . She could pity, or sacrifice herself, or have instincts' (p. 303). This gives two aspects of why it happened, Leonard as a representative of the suffering poor, and facets of Helen's nature. Anyway, can there be a wholly rational explanation of how two young people (however separated by class and convention) ended up in bed together?

vii Dolly

Dolly 'was a rubbishy little creature, and she knew it' (p. 101).

This short sentence about a minor character infuriated Angus Wilson: 'The concept that somebody can go round and be happy, that they can go round all their life and [Forster] didn't think that you should take them seriously, that he could accept that someone wouldn't be desperately unhappy if that was so, disturbs me.' So, 'I have rejected Forster's work. It is my absolute horror of the degree which, in his apparent embracing of his concern for those who are weak, those who don't have, those who are underprivileged and so on, that I find he can be so totally rejectful of human beings . . . *Howards End* is my idea of the book I really almost detest most. There are certain passages in that which I can't bear' (C. W. E. Bigsby, 'An Interview with Angus Wilson', *Literary Review*, 31 October 1980, pp. 8–9).

Yet the statement may be to make the reader sit up and say 'What!' Forster makes a strong statement looking out of the corner of his eye for the reaction. ('None of you girls have any nerves, really' (p. 202); 'When four men agree, what is a girl to do?' (p. 260); and of course 'We are not concerned with the very poor' (p. 58) are remarks of this kind). Neither need the line be Forster's; the novel certainly has passages with an implied narrator different from the name on the title-page, as will be discussed later.

Dolly may be 'rubbishy' to Wilcoxes: she is not a Wilcox, always 'Mrs Charles', and perhaps lacks their imperialist instincts. Charles grants her 'all his affection and half his attention' (p. 104) but 'no one noticed her' tears (p. 106). Lunching with Dolly, Margaret notices that 'It was evidently the custom to laugh at Dolly' (p. 199), damaging for any self-esteem she has. Indeed, Wilcoxes variously terrify, patronise, ignore, scold and contradict poor Dolly.

Note too that, while Dolly is forever placed by her name (as is Adolphus Cusins – usually 'Dolly' in *Major Barbara*), 'rubbishy' is the narrator's first word about her, and we need to be alert for change. Only 5 pages later she spots Charles contradicting himself about whether or not the note is in Mrs Wilcox's writing (p. 106). Later, as a harrassed mother relatively short of money, she begins 'to lose her brightness and good looks' (p. 259). More important, 'through Dolly, Margaret was destined to learn a good deal' (p. 203), about Miss Avery's wedding gifts (p. 260), the unpacking of her possessions at Howards End (p. 259), and finally about Mrs Wilcox's last wish for her house (p. 331) – this last would never have been revealed by a true Wilcox.

When we see how Dolly is treated by others, we stand back aghast – at them and at ourselves.

* * *

'How interesting that row of people was' comments Forster (p. 46) on the Schlegel party with Leonard beside them, in Queen's Hall listening to Beethoven's Fifth. 'Interesting' is one of Forster's slippery words: when we hear that Margaret found Leonard 'interesting on the whole – everyone interested the Schlegels on the whole at that time' (p. 50); 'to the Schlegels [Leonard] was an interesting creature' (p. 129); we are asked to see this as a limitation of the Schlegels. The bland word 'interesting' appears to understate the way Forster has the novelist's profound curiosity about people and their behaviour. Most of his characters do not divide into round and flat, in his own terminology; rather into major and minor, or predictable and surprising – and he enjoys the just-plausible surprise. Forster is not the kind of writer who is overtly a puppetmaster manipulating puppets. He can provide conventional description: Henry's 'complexion was robust, his hair had receded but not thinned' (p. 165). Yet Forster distances us from his creations by frequent authorial commenting and editorialising and by infrequent reminders that this is fiction, his occasional use of 'I', 'we' and 'the reader'. The novel has moments when a glass shade cuts off author from character, or character from reader, as glass doors of a lift separate Mrs Wilcox from Margaret (p. 95) and a 'glass shade' cuts off married couples from 'the world' (p. 254).

This section is written within the convention that fictional characters are to be judged as 'real people'. Two tests are applied: does this behaviour strike the reader as plausible, on his/her own experience of human beings (making the necessary leap to the conventions of another time) and does the novelist adequately explain and justify?

Such an approach now tends to look old-fashioned; neither is it appropriate to all novels.

3   Can a Feminist Like Forster?

A central paradox about E. M. Forster as a writer is his overwhelming interest in women.   (G. S. Amur, 1981, p. 24)

Margaret and Helen are both, in a limited and rather conventional way, feminists.   (Patricia Stubbs, 1979, p. 216)

The movement towards a female line of inheritance, together with the symbolic emasculation of the male figures, points to an endorsement of female power.   (Anne Wright, 1984, pp. 25–6)

Margaret and Helen are the major characters of the novel, and two other women, Mrs Wilcox and Miss Avery, embody strange, non-verbal, non-intellectual wisdom.

Margaret and Helen are thoughtful, highly intelligent, civilised, valuing the unseen and the inner life, and they also attempt practical benevolence. They employ a boot man because he is unemployed. Wilcoxes say 'Why be polite to servants? They don't understand it', and Schlegels reply, 'If they don't understand it, I do' (p. 38). Margaret wants to invite Leonard to tea after their first meeting at Queen's Hall. They mix with 'unshaven musicians, an actress even' (p. 29).

The Schlegels, however, go further than some familiar rather woolly idea of women as more sensitive. As single women leading their own lives, they have walked alone in the Appenines with rucksacks (p. 181). They are alert to the issues of their time. Helen has learned a faith in equality 'from poetry, or you', Margaret (p. 21). The big issues of the suffrage, independence, sexual freedom, the nature of marriage are all touched on here. Novels like Miles Franklin's *My Brilliant Career* and H. G. Wells' *Ann Veronica*, characters like Ann Whitfield in Bernard Shaw's *Man and Superman*, and Vivie in his *Mrs Warren's Profession*, Beatrice in James Joyce's *Exiles*, Clara in Lawrence's *Sons and Lovers* and his Ursula in *The Rainbow* raise these issues more stridently. Forster, as so often, is restrained and subdued, and only close reading shows that he both knows and cares.

Forster is true to the facts of time and class when there is no question of paid work for the Schlegels, or Dolly or Evie. Margaret tells Tibby that 'the desire for work . . . goes with a great deal that's bad, but in itself it's good, and I hope that for women, too, "not to work" will soon become as shocking as "not to be married" was a hundred years ago' (pp. 117–18). Bonnie Finkelstein comments on this speech: 'Margaret's belief in work is related to her attraction to Mr Wilcox, but it also expresses the heart of feminism . . . Margaret does not want to be a parasite of sex or of class' (1975, p. 94). Margaret's faith in work here resembles the outcries of Irina and Tusenbach a few years earlier in Anton Chekhov's *Three Sisters*.

Yet Margaret at work is going to the registry office to engage a housemaid, and flower-arranging with Aunt Juley, where Margaret talks while Juley works. In the final chapter, 'Margaret never stopped working' (p. 327), but even here her work is womens' work, sewing (p. 330). Lucy mends a sock on her honeymoon at the end of *A Room with a View*! Evie's various hobbies are an unintellectual alternative to Schlegel ways: exercise, making a rockery, dog-breeding, golf, tennis.

When Margaret gives a lunch party, Mrs Wilcox says: 'I sometimes think that it is wiser to leave action and discussion to men.' Margaret responds: 'Aren't we differing on something much wider, Mrs Wilcox? Whether women are to remain what they have been since the dawn of history; or whether, since men have moved forward so much, they too may move forward a little now. I say they may. I would even admit a biological change' (pp. 87–8). This remains an intriguing fragment, and – as usual with the younger Margaret – it is talk which she doesn't try to turn into action.

Margaret says early in the book that 'not to be married' is no longer a limitation, though the idea that 'old maids' are comic or pitiable lurks in her mind. Helen, too, can live unmarried: 'If I marry, it will either be a man who's strong enough to boss me or whom I'm strong enough to boss. So I shan't ever marry, for there aren't such men' (p. 195). Approaching her marriage, Margaret states a view of the married state which keeps proportion: 'She must remain herself, for his sake as well as her own, since a shadowy wife degrades the husband whom she accompanies; and she must assimilate for reasons of common honesty, since she had no right to marry a man and make him uncomfortable' (p. 220).

Her marriage, however, seems as conventional as those of Charles and Dolly and of Evie and Percy Cahill: the wife stays home and the husband goes out as breadwinner. Jacky is desperately anxious for the status and security she expects will come with marriage (p. 65). Paul, according to the assumptions of his class, can only marry when he has made money with which to support a wife (p. 35).

Margaret challenges male assumptions when the car approaching Oniton kills a child's cat, jumping out of the moving car to try to intervene: 'Why should the chauffeurs tackle the girl? Ladies sheltering behind men, men sheltering behind servants – the whole system's wrong, and she must challenge it' (p. 213). To Charles at this moment she is 'a woman in revolt' (p. 212). Yet, explaining her action, Margaret grovels to Henry. Before marriage, she is aware when she is manipulating Henry: 'She understood why some women prefer influence to rights. Mrs Plynlimmon, when condemning suffragettes, had said: "The woman who can't influence her husband to vote the way she wants ought to be ashamed of herself." Margaret had winced, but she was influencing Henry now, and though pleased at her little victory she knew that she had won it by the methods of the harem.' (p. 228).

Once she is married, she dwindles into a wife, becoming exactly what Henry wants and expects: 'He had only to call, and she clapped the book up and was ready to do what he wished' (p. 255) – though this is Henry's perception, and Margaret may have reluctantly put down the book.

Then comes her rebellion, when she puts her sister ahead of her husband. This is not merely choosing one relation over another, but is generalised as women versus men. Her revolt is in two stages. The first is when Helen comes to Howards End and Margaret defiantly prevents Henry coming into what is legally his house. 'A new feeling came over [Margaret]: she was fighting for women against men. She did not care about rights, but if men came into Howards End it should be over her body' (p. 283). Soon after Margaret stands with Helen in the drawing-room and observes that 'it's a room that men have spoiled through trying to make it nice for women. Men don't know what we want – .' Helen interjects, 'And never will', and Margaret, always less prone to extreme views, contradicts: 'I don't agree. In two thousand years they'll know' (p. 291): unhopeful for the women facing Henry that day!

Margaret's second revolt comes the same evening when she asks Henry's permission for her to spend the one night with Helen at Howards End. When Henry refuses, not only does she defy him, but she speaks her mind more forcefully than at any other time: 'A man who insults his wife when she's alive and cants with her memory when she's dead. A man who ruins a woman for his pleasure, and casts her off to ruin other men. And gives bad financial advice, and then says he is not responsible. These men are you. You can't recognize them, because you cannot connect. I've had enough of your unweeded kindness. I've spoilt you long enough. All your life you have been spoilt. Mrs Wilcox spoiled you. No one has ever told you what you are – muddled, criminally muddled' (p. 300). K. W. Gransden describes this speech as 'one of the finest and deadliest pieces of feminism to have been written in the era of the suffragettes . . . [Henry] inherited a man's world; he has always commanded; he has always been obeyed. When he took her out to lunch, he told her what to eat . . . When Margaret attacks, she attacks with her head as well as her heart and what she says is ruthless and unanswerable' (1962, p. 72). When Margaret afterwards reflects calmly, she is proud of what she said: 'Her speech to him seemed perfect. She would not have altered a word. It had to be uttered once in a life, to adjust the lopsidedness of the world. It was spoken not only to her husband, but to thousands of men like him – a protest against the inner darkness in high places that comes with a commercial age' (p. 322).

Something between victory for Margaret and reconciliation follows. Finally women hold power domestically. Personally, Margaret acts on what the Chelsea discussion group considered years before: she contributes to the re-distribution of wealth by giving away half her money. The women take no role in opposing war, protecting the countryside from the spread of suburbia, or in business (Paul continues capitalist exploitation). Insofar as Howards End and its grounds represent the nation, on the level of myth, the women have finally triumphed.

Patricia Stubbs concludes that 'Forster fails in *Howards End* because he accepts the traditionally rigid separation between male and female psychological characteristics. Wilcoxes and Schlegels are the product of highly conventional ideas of masculinity and feminity; the men are defined entirely in terms of the outside world which orthodox opinion still believes was their natural sphere, and the women are restricted to the private "inner" world of the emotions . . . All this really adds up to is a superficial modernity; fundamentally Forster is still living in Ruskin's ideal world where men are naturally outgoing and aggressive and women inward-looking and affectionate' (1979, pp. 219–20). Jonah Raskin makes the point more forcefully: Forster 'thinks he is celebrating women through the Schlegels by making them sensitive, well-educated and imaginative. But he only maintains the same stereotypes women have always been cast in' (1971, p. 252).

The women of *Howards End* are not doers. The Schlegels, single or married, will not be active suffragettes or crusading journalists, will not set out to become doctors or lawyers. Forster is not picturing such pioneering women: there were few in 1910, and Forster can be faulted only by the most fervent late twentieth century feminist for not making Margaret and Helen more feminist than they were.

Margaret defies men when push comes to shove. Otherwise, women in the novel are to be valued for a kind of sense deeper and richer than men are capable of.

Once the narrator does challenge 'highly conventional ideas of masculinity and feminity'. This is on the train journey from London to the wedding at Oniton, where the Fussells, father and son, accompany Margaret, a small girl and four other women. 'Nothing could have exceeded the kindness of the two men. They raised the windows for some ladies, and lowered them for others, they rang the bell for the servant, they identified the colleges as the train slipped past Oxford, they caught books or bag-purses in the act of tumbling on the floor. Yet there was nothing finicky about their politeness: it had the Public School touch, and, though sedulous, was virile.' Males here are conventionally courteous to females. Margaret questions this but, trying hard to be Wilcox-like, 'said nothing when the Oxford colleges were identified wrongly'. Then the narrator slips in a radical, though brief, note of doubt: '"Male and female created He them"; the journey to Shrewsbury confirmed this questionable statement' (p. 209).

Forster in this novel shows he dislikes class distinctions, and in *A Passage to India* he attacks racism. Thus he also understood something of how women are oppressed in a patriarchal society, and in marriage. He is a fellow-travelling moderate feminist, enlightened for a man in his time.

4 Can a Marxist Like Margaret?

Howards End 'is a story of the class war. The war is latent but actual – so actual indeed that a sword is literally drawn and a man is really killed.'   (Trilling, 1944, p. 102)

It is important to recognize that [Forster] shares with Marx the fundamental premise that 'life is not determined by consciousness, but consciousness by life'.   (Suzette A. Henke, 1986, pp. 117–18)

If bourgeois norms reduce all relationships to exchange values, then personal relationships must be devalued ... It is a large component in Galsworthy's description of the Forsytes in *The Man of Property* (1906), and of E. M. Forster's description of the Wilcoxes, 'the world of telegrams and anger', *Howards End*'.   (Joan Rockwell, 1974, p. 94)

Forster 'is incapable of understanding the lower-middle classes. He is frightened of them ... It is Forster's crippling defect that he is unable to imagine revolutionary alternatives ... He is reactionary, counterrevolutionary in content and form.'   (Jonah Raskin, 1971, pp. 245, 250, 252)

Some of the criticism of *Howards End* turns on Forster's own upper middle class position, dependent – like the Schlegels – on unearned income, and of writing – like most novelists – of the middle class. He explains of the Schlegel sisters, 'in their own fashion they cared deeply about politics, though not as politicians would have us care; they desired that public life should mirror whatever is good in the life within' (p. 41). This may be true of Forster, yet he seems more uneasy about injustice and inequality, to see the problem as more urgent, personal and immediate – yet also cautiously to shrink from radical solutions.

Twice politics are placed as trivial beside beautiful, timeless Nature. The drive from Shrewsbury to Oniton prompts this from the narrator, so responsive to landscapes: 'Quiet mysteries were in progress behind those tossing horizons: the west, as ever, was retreating with some secret which may not be worth the discovery, but which no practical man will ever discover. They spoke of Tariff Reform . . . Margaret playfully confessed herself on the other side, and they began to quote from their respective handbooks while the motor carried them deeper into the hills' (pp. 210–11). Similarly, Margaret walks to Howards End through the different kind of beauty of Hertfordshire: 'Though its contours were slight, there was a touch of freedom in their sweep to which Surrey will never attain, and the distant brow of the Chilterns towered like a mountain. "Left to itself", was Margaret's opinion, "this county would vote Liberal"' (p. 263). This appears as a rare case in the book where Margaret's sensitivity is faulted: the true Margaret would dwell on the beauty, not think about voting – but at this point she is attempting much of the time to be a conforming Wilcox.

The novel has six references to socialism, two to a millionaire denouncing it (pp. 117, 155); one to Aunt Juley being suspicious of it (p. 72); one, predictably, to Henry arguing that attending to social problems 'in too many cases . . . leads to morbidity, discontent and socialism' (p. 151). The other two references are by Margaret. At the womens' discussion group she argues for the need of the Basts and the millions like them for money now, though 'when your socialism comes it may be different, and we may think in terms of commodities instead of cash' (pp. 133–4). Margaret identifies with socialists debating with Henry about whether equality could last: 'My socialists do. Yours mayn't; but I strongly suspect yours of not being socialists, but ninepins, which you have constructed for your won amusement.' Henry retorts only 'I don't care' (p. 160). This is the only time when Margaret is shown disagreeing about ideas with Henry, though later we read that, from Henry's perspective, when they debate, 'once or twice she had him in quite a tight corner, but as soon as he grew really serious she gave in' (p. 255).

The novel supplies no answer to the problem of poverty, even of the Basts specifically; poverty remains a debating society topic (Chapter 15). Leonard would be happier had he not been torn from his rural roots, but a permanent return (as opposed to a walk through the woods at night, and his final dawn walk from Hilton station to Howards End) is not practicable. The ruling class can be blamed for the Basts' situation: Henry's affair with Jacky and his offhand wrong advice which dooms Leonard. More positively, trust: Leonard can be left alone in the Wickham Place drawing-room with the much-cherished painting by Ricketts: Margaret says of their father: 'You remember how he would trust strangers, and if they fooled him he would say, "It's better to be fooled than to be suspicious" – that the confidence trick is the work of man, but the want-of-confidence trick is the work of the devil' (p. 55). The line is repeated when Margaret is guilty of agreeing to the trap for Helen at Howards End: 'She had first to purge a greater crime than any that Helen could have committed – that want of confidence that is the work of the devil' (p. 286). This connection across more than 200 pages is one of the dozens likely to be noticed at a third or fourth reading. Yet the Schlegel's father could afford to be fooled a few times, as Forster established a few pages earlier: 'To trust people is a luxury in which only the wealthy can indulge; the poor cannot afford it' (p. 48). Finally, the Basts can be given money. Margaret talks of this at the discussion group; Helen tries to give Leonard £5,000 and he refuses it; at the end Margaret is giving away half her income.

The Schlegels are honest and straightforward in seeing their dependence on a private income. Margaret explains to Aunt Juley: 'I'm tired of these rich people who pretend to be poor, and think it shows a nice mind to ignore the piles of money that keep their feet above the waves. I stand each year upon six hundred pounds, and Helen upon the same, and Tibby will stand upon eight, and as fast as our pounds crumble away into the sea they are renewed – from the sea, yes, from the sea. And all our thoughts are the thoughts of six-hundred-pounders, and all our speeches' (p. 72). This clear-sightedness about her situation leads to her recognition of the need for Wilcoxes: 'If Wilcoxes hadn't worked and died in England for thousands of years, you and I couldn't sit here without having our throats cut. There would be no trains, no ships to carry us literary people about in, no fields even. Just savagery . . . More and more do I refuse to draw my income and sneer at those who guarantee it' (pp. 177–8).

(Just what £600 amounted to in 1910 is now hard to determine. Added to the incomes of Helen and Tibby, it is enough for a sizeable house in a respectable part of London with some servants. Six hundred a year is much less than the wealth of the millionaire who owns the London house and of Henry, 'whose fortune was not so very far below' that of a millionaire (p. 139). His plan for a house in Midhurst with 'a good many gables' and four tennis courts (p. 258) must be a house fit for a millionaire).

Margaret's directness about her money is shown when she tries to discuss their future with Henry immediately after they become engaged. 'How much have you a year?' she asks. He evades and she presses: 'Don't you know your income? Or don't you want to tell it me?' Recalling the kind of person Henry is, she backs off with 'Don't tell me. I don't want to know' (p. 182). The Wilcoxes are obliquely faulted for insensitivity when Margaret hears they give the servants money as Christmas presents (p. 90); presumably the Schlegels painstakingly choose appropriate presents. Yet Helen's attempt to give £5,000 to Leonard is also reducing personal relationships to banknotes.

Margaret's 'How much have you a year?' is an important question. Two other questions are explored throughout the novel. Mrs Wilcox's question, 'Why do people who have enough money try to get more money?' (p. 99) is less naïve than the Wilcoxes think it to be. 'How ought I to dispose of my money?' (p. 132) is equally crucial.

Some critics have seen Forster as endorsing Margaret's thinking: be realistic about your income, and then you can be complacent afterwards. D. S. Savage sees the book as 'a justification of economic privilege' (1950, p. 58). Paul Delany similarly sees the work as 'a justification of [Forster's] economic status' (1988, p. 287). Forster alternatively, is descriptive, not approving, as Claude Summers puts it: 'Among the novel's genuine distinctions is its honest recognition of money as the basis of modern society' (1983, p. 114). Cedric Watts is more decisive: '*Howards End* is an astonishingly deliberate and self-aware experiment in the demystification and remystification of money' (1990, p. 153). The novel becomes more typical of Forster if seen as his worrying about his good fortune to be born to money. Forster boldly grasps a society based on money, then expresses discomfort rather than putting forward solutions.

The narrator asks Margaret to be generous to Henry 'considering all that the business mind has done for England' (p. 184). As so often, the reader has to pause and ask whether this is ironic. What Forster repeatedly shows is that the business mind is less wrong than limited.

Forster also deals with property ownership, and its responsibilities. Margaret is angry that the millionaire is going to demolish their house to build flats. She does not try to form a preservation society (in 1907 Forster had given money to the campaign to save the mansion, Battersea Rise, which had been the home of his aunt, Marianne Thornton, but the campaign failed). Neither does Margaret reconcile herself to the inevitable, but instead refuses to think about it: 'What right had such men – but Margaret checked herself. That way lies madness' (p. 117). Henry only once sees a connection, and this is between his refusal to let Helen sleep at Howards End and owning property, telling Charles: 'To my mind this question is connected with something far greater, the rights of property itself' (p. 317). Putting property before human feelings is Wilcoxian. Howards End comes to the owner who can best appreciate it. This is a Brechtian conclusion: the child Michael goes to the best mother, not the birth mother, in *The Caucasian Chalk Circle*: in the last line the Singer bequeathes 'the valley to the waterers, that it shall bear fruit'. The meadow at Howards End will continue to provide hay, not go under a 'red rust'. Forster conscientiously wrestles with the problems of ownership in his essay of 1926, 'My Wood'. He bought a small wood with his earnings from sales of *A Passage to India*, 'the first property that I have owned'. So he meditates on the psychology of ownership, choosing to leave aside the larger issue of 'the effect of private ownership upon the community'. He finds that ownership 'makes me feel heavy. Property does have this effect. Property produces men of weight . . . Property makes its owner feel that he ought to do something to it. Yet he isn't sure what. A restlessness comes over him . . . We have not yet learned to manage our materialism and carnality properly; they are still entangled with the desire for ownership' (*Abinger Harvest*, 1936, pp. 22–5). All this he had intuited in the character of Henry Wilcox, long before he was himself a man of property.

In making the Schlegels half-German, Forster makes them cosmopolitan and thus alien to the proudly English Wilcoxes, though – ironically – the families have first met at Speyer, in Germany. More important, the Schlegels embody the case for the absurdity of a war between Britain and Germany, a growing threat after the international crises of 1905 and 1908, with expansionist countries opposed in Morocco and the Balkans. The rivalry some-times appears playful and harmless. Aunt Juley wants the German relatives 'to hear what we are doing in music' (p. 49), which happens to be Elgar's 'Pomp and Circumstance'; Forster knows this cannot compare with Beethoven's Fifth Symphony. Much of the lunch party for Mrs Wilcox is spent comparing British and German love of beauty and liberty of thought (pp. 85–7). Instead of admiring the view from the Purbeck Hills, Frieda Mosebach annoys Aunt Juley by claiming that the hills of Pomerania and Friedrich Wilhelms Bad, by the Baltic, are superior (p. 171). A clergyman lunching at Simpson's in the Strand is overheard remarking: 'Their Emperor wants war; well, let him have it' (p. 158). One of the few times when Forster speaks unmistakeably in his own voice is in the editorial: 'The remark "England and Germany are bound to fight" renders war a little more likely each time that is made, and is therefore made the more readily by the gutter press of each nation' (p. 74) – echoes of the hate-Saddam-Hussein mood of Autumn 1990 and its consequences.

Howards End comments on imperialism, which will be Forster's central subject later in *A Passage to India*. Wales, England's first conquest, can be seen from Oniton, the river flows down from there and 'the tower chimes "See the Conquering Hero"' (p. 246). The Schlegels' stocks are in foreign companies and they lose money on Home Rails.

Paul Wilcox works in Nigeria, although, according to Margaret 'it is beastly work – dull country, dishonest natives, an eternal fidget over fresh water and food' (p. 119). Colonel Fussell is Indian Army (p. 80), two of the Oniton wedding guests are Anglo-Indian (p. 208), Charles has brought back a Dutch Bible from the Boer

War (p. 167). Henry himself works with the Imperial and West African Rubber Company (rubber associates with the tyres of the cars the Wilcoxes like and which Margaret hates). On the office wall is a map 'on which the whole continent [of Africa] appeared, looking like a whale marked out for blubber' (p. 196). That this map is significant is emphasised when Margaret, in Howards End of all places, thinks of it again: 'She thought of the map of Africa; of empires; of her father; of the two supreme nations, streams of whose life warmed her blood, but, mingling, had cooled her brain' (p. 202). Delany points out that 'the reader is surely meant to think of Gillray's famous cartoon of Napoleon and Pitt carving up the world like a Christmas pudding', 'The Plumb-Pudding in Danger' of 1805 (1988, p. 289). This is likely because Gillrays hang in Henry's house in Ducie Street (p. 167). Balanced Margaret admits to Tibby that 'an Empire bores me, so far, but I can appreciate the heroism that builds it up' (p. 119). The last word on imperialism, however, is a much harsher one: 'The Imperialist is not what he thinks or seems. He is a destroyer' (p. 315).

Forster acknowledged his limited, under-informed, pre-World War I social views much later, in his essay of 1946, 'The Challenge of our Time':

I belong to the fag-end of Victorian liberalism, and can look back to an age whose challenges were moderate in their tone, and the cloud on whose horizon was no bigger than a man's hand. In many ways it was an admirable age. It practised benevolence and philanthropy, was humane and intellectually curious, upheld free speech, had little colour-prejudice, believed that individuals are and should be different, and entertained a sincere faith in the progress of society. The world was to become better and better, chiefly through the spread of parliamentary institutions. The education I received in those far-off and fantastic days made me soft and I am very glad it did, for I have seen plenty of hardness since, and I know it does not even pay . . .

Though the education was humane it was imperfect, inasmuch as we none of us realized our economic position. In came the nice fat dividends, up rose the lofty thoughts, and we did not realize that all the time we were exploiting the poor of our own country and the backward races abroad, and getting bigger profits from our investments than we should. We refused to face this unpalatable truth. I remember being told as a small boy, 'Dear, don't talk about money, it's ugly' – a good example that of Victorian defence mechanism.

All that has changed in the present century. The dividends have shrunk to decent proportions and have in some cases disappeared. The poor have kicked. The backward races are kicking – and more power to their boots. Which means that life has become less comfortable for the Victorian liberal, and that our outlook, which seems to me admirable, has lost the basis of golden sovereigns upon which it originally rose, and now hangs over the abyss.   (*Two Cheers for Democracy*, 1965, pp. 67–8)

Forster himself provides a shrewd account of what *Howards End* left out – because of his own ignorance and failures in understanding, and of all those around him.

5   Who is Telling us the Story?

We are prompted to ask if the narrator of *Howards End*, although calling attention to himself, avoids destroying the 'illusion and nobility' of the novel. Are his essays and commentaries integral to the work? Do they serve a purpose, or are they merely the undisciplined ramblings of an author who, having written essays since 1900, cannot help but riddle his novel with authorial comment?   (Paul R. Rivenberg, 1982, p. 168)

Despite the narrator's brilliance, his persuasion must ultimately be regarded as unsuccessful . . . His reflections are often disconnected from the action, so that the novel appears to present an uneven alternation between essay and scene, comment and action. To a degree found in no other Forster novel, the narrator's diction is abstract, metaphorical, hyperbolical; the anxiety and inflation of his tone suggest the desperation of his attempt to harmonize and persuade.   (Barbara Rosecrance, 1982, p. 134)

Forster clearly has a distinctive and idiosyncratic voice or tone in the novel. Yet critics until the last 20 years have been content to state this, without further scrutiny.

In fact Forster in *Aspects of the Novel* had revealed something of his own practice: 'The whole intricate question of method resolves itself not into formulae but into the power of the writer to bounce the reader into accepting what he says . . . This power to expand and contract perception (of which the shifting viewpoint is a symptom), this right to intermittent knowledge – I find it one of the great advantages of the novel-form, and it has a parallel in our perception of life. We are stupider at some times than others; we can enter into people's minds occasionally but not always, because our minds get tired; and this intermittence lends in the long run variety and colour to the experiences we receive. A quantity of novelists, English novelists especially, have behaved like this to the people in their books: played fast and loose with them, and I cannot see why they should be censured' (1976, pp. 81–4).

One may as well begin with 'one may as well begin', the first line. This carries the implication that the story might have begun at some other point, such as the first meeting of Schlegels and Wilcoxes, and that a mind has determined what is to be revealed, in what order. 'One' pitches the narrator halfway between an invisible storyteller and the directness of 'I'. The controlling intelligence intervenes again in the first letter, with three '[omission]'s, editing out irrelevant detail of ladies' evening dress, while also attracting attention to the intrusion.

Early in the second chapter, as Margaret and Aunt Juley discuss Helen's letter, the text goes: 'Margaret was silent. If her aunt could not see why she must go down [to Howards End], she was not going to tell her. She was not going to say: "I love my dear sister; I must be near her at this crisis of her life." The affections are more reticent than the passions, and their expression more subtle. If she herself should ever fall in love with a man, she, like Helen, would proclaim it from the house-tops' (p. 24). Here an omniscient narrator takes the reader into Margaret's mind, steps out to comment that 'the affections are more reticent than the passions', then goes back into Margaret's thoughts. Margaret might well reflect this herself at some point, but not in the middle of a tense breakfast with Aunt Juley. These shifts from character to narrator's commentary and reflections happen frequently (e.g., Margaret thinks of Christmas, p. 91), even as an interjection in the middle of a sentence: 'Bursts of disloyal laughter – you must remember that they are half German – greeted these suggestions' (p. 57). Or this: 'The serious parts of the discussion had been of higher merit than the playful – in a men's debate is the reverse more general? – but the meeting broke up hilariously enough' (p. 135). (The question dropped into the middle is addressed to the male reader, in fact one familiar with the conventions of a Cambridge Union debate).

The last page of Chapter 2 moves briskly through a range of first, second and third persons, singular and plural:

> Margaret had strong feelings about the various railway termini. They are *our* gates to the glorious and the unknown. Through them *we* pass out into adventure and sunshine, to them, alas! *we* return . . . He is a chilly Londoner who does not endow *his* stations with some personality . . . To Margaret – *I* hope that it will not set *the reader* against her – the station of King's Cross had always suggested infinity . . . If *you* think this ridiculous, remember that it is not Margaret who is telling *you* about it; and let *me* hasten to add that they were in plenty of time for the train.   (p. 27 [my italics])

Forster here prepares for the extraordinary range from the utterly mundane to the very high-flown which he will constantly display, and allows for the possibility of Margaret speaking to the reader. Further, he sets up a most complex relationship, in which the narrator can be 'I' or 'we' and the audience can be brought in as 'we', 'you' and 'the reader'. Forster teases: sometimes he is himself, sometimes disguised. For readers who have a sense of his personality, his guard goes up and down: clearly a persona, then perhaps a persona, then almost certainly Forster himself. The reader can be mocked, even seen as outside the sympathies of the author, in the reaction to Leonard's report of his all-night walk: 'You may laugh at him, you who have slept nights out on the veldt, with your rifle beside you and all the atmosphere of adventure pat. And you also may laugh who think adventures silly. But do not be surprised if Leonard is shy whenever he meets you' (p. 131). Meeting a fictional character is postulated here: playful, or helping to draw us into belief in the reality of Leonard?

The reader who sleeps out on the veldt and the reader who laughs at adventures are just two possible readers. The implied reader varies: sometimes to be English is required; sometimes

belonging to a knowing Cambridge/Bloomsbury ingroup; sometimes with spare cash for a concert ticket: 'You are bound
to admit that such a noise is cheap at two shillings' (p. 45).
Malcolm Bradbury stresses the point of all that surrounds story and
character: '*Howards End* is a novel in which the events themselves
are less important than the apparatus by which they are perceived
and interpreted' (1962, p. 231). Andrew Wright speaks not of the
whole 'apparatus' but of the significant relationship established
between writer and reader: 'The focus of *Howards End* is less
on what happens to the characters than on the outcome of the
repeatedly defined relation between Forster and his audience. As
a story-teller Forster is easy and informal, sympathetic, expectant,
allusive, intimate' (1987, p. 59). Paul Rivenberg makes a useful
analogy for what Forster does: 'His contact with the reader must
be direct, as it is in his essays. In *Howards End*, just as Margaret tries
to break down the wall Mr Wilcox has built to protect his emotions,
Forster tries to break down the wall between the narrator and the
reader. He tries to connect directly with his audience through
both interjected essays and brief, disruptive comments' (1982,
pp. 174–5).

The narrator readily acknowledges the mechanics of story-
telling: 'To follow it is unnecessary. It is rather a moment when
the commentator should step forward' (p. 107). 'Explanations
were difficult at this stage, and Leonard was too silly – or, it is
tempting to write, too sound a chap to attempt them' (p. 130). 'It
is convenient to follow him in the discharge of his duties' (p. 252).
This is the Forster who admitted in *Aspects of the Novel*, 'Yes – oh dear
yes – the novel tells a story' (p. 53).

Often the narrator is omniscient. He knows about the entire lives
of the characters, even after the end of the book, as in: 'To Helen,
at all events, her life was to bring nothing more intense than the
embrace of this boy who played no part in it' (p. 39). Similarly,
of Margaret and Oniton, 'she never saw it again' (p. 246). Henry
'would settle down – though [Margaret] could not realize this'
(p. 323). Omniscience, however, is lacking about Mrs Wilcox:
'Perhaps it was she who had desired the Miss Schlegels to be
invited to *Howards End* . . . All this is speculation: Mrs Wilcox has
left few clear indications behind her' (p. 75). More surprisingly,
the narrator is suddenly uninformed about Helen: Margaret 'does
understand herself, she has some rudimentary control over her own

growth. Whether Helen has succeeded one cannot say' (p. 273). Douglas H. Thomson concludes that 'Forster anticipates the questioning of omniscience that distinguishes the narratives of his later contemporaries, such as Joyce and Woolf' (1983, p. 131).

Margaret 'can be said to speak for Forster', claimed Wilfred Stone in *The Cave and the Mountain* (1966, p. 235). Margaret says that Helen's feeling for Paul is 'dead', and a comment contradicting Margaret follows: she 'was making a most questionable statement – that any emotion, any interest, once vividly aroused, can wholly die' (p. 69). This extraordinary implied narrator can even write as a woman, with an 'us' apparently limited to females: 'Pity, if one may generalize, is at the bottom of woman. When men like us, it is for our better qualities, and however tender their liking we dare not be unworthy of it, or they will quietly let us go. But unworthiness stimulates woman' (p. 240). From this paragraph Kinley Roby postulates that the persona of the narrator is a woman, a secret kept till the end of Chapter 28 (1972, pp. 116–24). Roby sees four qualities of this woman, who is decisive, 'critical of the quality of modern life', sententious and 'a romantic'. While this idea has not found favour, if the narrator is seen as quite separate from Forster, some difficulties are removed – the triviality of 'Life is a mysterious business' (p. 32) and the unease aroused by 'We are not concerned with the very poor' and 'Dolly was a rubbishy little creature, and she knew it'.

Struggling to catch and label Forster's narrative voice, J. L. Van De Vyvere categorised 'two broad tendencies': 'The first, the traditional mode, is probably the legacy of Forster's great admiration for Jane Austen, while the second, subjective and individualised, is doubtless an expression of the author's high regard for the value of the personal voice. The resulting overall proportion achieved in the narrative voice creates a unique mediatorial quality which has a powerful effect on the reader. This third note, the dynamic center which moves between the two tendencies, is the shadow of Forster, the author, at work amidst his creation' (1976, pp. 205–6). Cedric Watts is more accurate when he identifies the multiplicity of notes struck: 'Even when the point of view is clearly that of the narrator, the voice shifts markedly from the coolly detached to the warmly sympathetic, from the ironic or satiric to the enthusiastic, and from the prosaic to the lyrical' (1990, p. 155). Kenneth Graham, a very careful reader, concludes that Forster has suffered from being seen as a clear-cut essayist in his fiction – 'a truly civilized mind', and the like – rather than as an edgy and elusive explorer-through-process, whose words, even at their most apparently discursive, form part of a larger and qualifying, even twisting, dialectic of plot and image, and are always on the point of being controverted, twitched on to their backs, by his creative mental habit of disclaiming . . . So Forster, who as a moralist esteems 'connection', as a narrator and symbolist deliberately follows words into the places where no connection is possible . . . The naturalistic and the highly stylized are in perpetual interplay, so that the reader is in a state of surprise and restlessness – a state of aesthetic response that then finds its conceptual equivalent within Forster's view of the world. (1988, pp. 154, 155, 160)

Some of the narrator's interjections are banal: 'Life is a mysterious business' is worthy only of Aunt Juley – or Jacky. Forster can write as an essayist, with all the time in the world, in the tones of a G. K. Chesterton or Max Beerbohm turning out a leisurely column for a weekly: 'There is something continental about Chelsea Embankment. It is an open space used rightly, a blessing more frequent in Germany than here' (p. 135). Forster can be a reflective old clubman, suggesting a person much older than he was at the time of writing, 30: 'While the gods are powerful, we learn little about them' (p. 145). There is editorialising, prompted by farm labourers at Hilton. 'They kept the life of daylight. They are England's hope. Clumsily they carry forward the torch of the sun' (p. 314). Also, and conspicuously, the poetic; the most over-written sentence in the novel is: 'Spring had come, clad in no classical garb, yet fairer than all springs; fairer even than she who walks through the myrtles of Tuscany with the graces before her and the zephyr behind' (p. 264).

The variety of voices and the changes of tone have two effects. Francis Gillen rightly sees that the narrator takes the reader away from 'a purely realistic interpretation of events' (1970, p. 149). Jonathan Raban presents an equally important consequence: 'Forster gives a superb demonstration of the power and flexibility of bounced narrative, blending the possibilities of both omnisicience and the limited point of view . . . What does Forster really think of Helen Schlegel or Leonard Bast? . . . In bounced narrative the reader has to make up his own mind about the characters' (1968, p. 36).

Understanding the full complexity of voice in the novel has probably just begin. For a start, one might look at each use of 'I', 'you', 'we', 'one' and the like not to count them but to decide just what effect is achieved each time.

6   Are the Modes Mixed?

Speaking roughly, we may divide [novelists] into the preachers and the teachers, headed by Tolstoy and Dickens, on the one hand, and the pure artists, headed by Jane Austen and Turgenev, on the other. Mr Forster, it seems, has a strong impulse to belong to both camps at once.   (Virginia Woolf, 1927, p. 345)

A number of different genres are forcefully yoked together in Forster's cumbersome fictional structure: comedy of manners, medieval romance, allegory, and naturalistic drama. The astonishing edifice is baroque and unwieldy.   (Suzette A. Henke, 1986, p. 117)

Howards End 'smoothly manipulates imagery and symbolism, plot and character, into an organic whole. In so doing, it gracefully integrates social comedy, metaphysical explorations, and political concerns'.   (Claude J. Summers, p. 138)

Two external factors have led to exaggeration of the non-realist element in Forster. Forster as mystic comes from taking some playful early short stories – 'The Story of a Panic', 'The Other Kingdom' – too seriously; *The Longest Journey* blatantly moves beyond everyday reality. Further, his *Aspects of the Novel* has two unexpected sections, on Fantasy and Prophecy, showing these are important for him. Insofar as Forster is writing 'comedy of manners' or 'Social comedy' he is writing broadly in the manner of most novelists of the previous hundred years, but if he can be shown to be introducing other elements, he becomes innovative, associated with Modernism, looking more into the twentieth century than back to the nineteenth. Peter Keating phrases Forster's position thus: 'The self-conscious symbolism and the strain of mysticism in the novel demonstrates his additional distrust of realism, but Forster clung to realism with a desperation that makes *Howards End* one of the great representative novels of the age' (1989, p. 325). I question how 'self-conscious' the symbolism is and the issue can equally be phrased the other way, that Forster wanted to go, from time to time, beyond realism, to introduce symbolism and mysticism. The issue for Peter Widdowson is 'vision juxtaposed with reality' (1977, p. 98) which overstates the amount of space actually devoted to anything which could be described as 'vision'. Anne Wright finds the work 'uneasily poised between realism and symbolism' (1984, p. 24) yet fails to show why the poise is uneasy. John Beer has no difficulty because 'Howards End is the main link between a realistic plot which can be grasped at one reading and a pattern of symbolism' (1962, p. 101).

Most of the novel is written in the convention that the novel tells a story about carefully observed people – in the time and place of the readers. Aunt Juley (who almost runs away with novel) and Frieda Mosebach are figures purely of social comedy. Chapter 3 (Aunt Juley vs Charles) is entertaining; as the novel continues, the confrontations grow more serious: the two scenes of Schlegels with Leonard and the visit from Jacky (Chs. 13, 14, 16) have more seriousness because of the pathos of Leonard and because the two sides are unequal; Charles visiting Tibby would be most comic were the issues less important (Ch. 39).

The most obvious break in the convention is the kinds of authorial intrusion discussed in the previous section. After this, the reader identifies other elements. Walter Allen had a single label and was bluntly dismissive: Forster attempted 'a mingling of social comedy and poetry . . . the poetry doesn't work' (1958, p. 337). The 'poetry' is actually what is often disparagingly called 'fine writing' or 'purple passages', of a kind less bad than unfashionable. Forster is careful to keep these short: what Hertfordshire in Springtime is like is part of his subject, and even then he changes to entertaining us with the pretentions of Madge in the middle to avoid much of an essay or even extended description (pp. 262–4). The most ambitious passage of this kind, in Chapter 19, is long opening and closing paragraphs with a great deal of dialogue, first frivolous and then earnest, between. What Allen calls 'poetry' is unusual in the novel, and may be dated, but I note only that it 'doesn't work' for Allen.

Other elements are symbolism, discussed in Part 2; the vision of the last chapter; and mysticism, though such a line as 'We are evolving, in ways that Science cannot measure, to ends that Theology does not contemplate' (p. 238) has more to do with the Theosophy in which Margaret dabbles (pp. 158, 257) than with Forster's philosophy. When Helen pours water over the dead Leonard (p. 316) this can be taken as a posthumous baptism, and as an addition to the pattern of moving water which flows through the book, but – only five words – this is hardly an awkward intrusion.

Such forms are neither 'integrated' (Summers) nor 'forcefully yoked together' (Henke). At times the elements-beyond-realism are blended; mostly, they are juxtaposed or mingled. Forster follows the direction of his epigraph, 'only connect', not fuse, or fuse only in the last chapter. Few readers, surely, are troubled by Forster's story occasionally reaching beyond the everyday, and having symbolic underpinning.

7   The End: Conclusion or Confusion?

Nearly all novels are feeble at the end. This is because the plot requires to be wound up.   (E. M. Forster, *Aspects of the Novel*, pp. 93–4)

Forster achieves at the last, not proportion, but the halfway meeting of opposites that Margaret deplores . . . The solution is, at the best, unsteady, at the worst, facile.   (Alan Wilde, 1964, p. 123)

The novel, like the symphony, ends in joyous splendor – and for the same reason. Forster chooses to make all right in the end. But the goblins are there. Panic and emptiness, squalor and tragedy – they may return, indeed, they will. And they have a place in the splendor and triumph.   (George H. Thomson, 1967, p. 198)

The last chapter is controversial. Is this a happy ending? Or is it a happy ending symbolically but not realistically, or the other way round? Does the end balance some achievements with some limitations?

The title directs readers to be attentive to the end. 'I'm ended' says Henry just before the last chapter (p. 324), yet he is not, as he survives in the following chapter. More cryptically, Helen echoes him (p. 327) yet she is excited as she cries 'we've seen to the very end' (p. 332) of the cutting of the hay. The title, writes Daniel R. Schwarz, 'becomes a pun on death and destruction, a pun that reverberates throughout the novel' (1989, p. 129). The title, in fact, asks whether the values of Ruth Howard can be passed on beyond her lifetime, then answers Yes in the last pages.

The massed ranks of commentators differ both about whether or not the ending can be seen as happy, and about whether or not the ending is convincing. Two teams of five:

AGAINST

At the end of ... *Howards End*, Margaret Schlegel is no nearer understanding or being understood by the Wilcoxes.   (Francis Gillen, 1970, p. 140)

Howards End is 'a sappy, sentimental book. Forster wants us to go away feeling all warm and soft and mushy inside.'   (Jonah Raskin, 1971, p. 242)

The close of the book can hardly escape being found, in its innocent way, sentimental.   (F. R. Leavis, 1952, p. 271)

The concluding joy that reigns at Howards End is fragile and qualified.   (Douglass H. Thomson, 1983, p. 131)

The final scene in the hay is pure fantasy, a sentimental hope for the future for which the action of the plot has given no support. The union of the child of liberal idealism and underprivileged effort, taking over the heritage of the earth, is a dream.   (C. B. Cox, 1963, p. 93)

FOR

[The novel ends on] a synthesis, though perhaps uneasily achieved, but a synthesis nevertheless. (David Shusterman, 1965, p. 157)

The finding at the end of the novel is affirmative – for civilization. Forster discovers or reveals it to be fragile and perpetually
endangered but, surprisingly enough, strong enough to with-
stand what might look to be fatal blows. Forster as narrator of
the book has promised this astonishing prospect. His revelation
is that intelligence is strong enough, that personal relations can
endure, that culture can survive the collision with the anarchy
of panic and emptiness, that love can succeed. The close of
Howards End is idyllic, a joyous tableau, at once prophetic and
fabulous.   (Andrew Wright, 1987, pp. 72–3)

In the closing pages of the book we see Margaret enjoying an idyllically bucolic time with her sister and the sister's
son.   (Cedric Watts, 1990, p. 157)

The final scene convinces: the prose and the passion are truly
both 'exalted', and 'human love' is 'seen at its height'. The final
vision is androgynous, and it is crucially important that no one,
and no one sex, 'controls' anything.   (Bonnie Finkelstein, 1975,
p. 92)

[The end] provides a sense of resolution and continuity in
Margaret's moral triumph, the birth of Helen and Leonard's
son . . . the abundant hay crop – a sense that, at least this once,
the living and the dead may be at one and at peace.   (Alan
Warren Friedman, 1987, p. 107)

Surveying such differences among critics, these questions arise: Is
the difference simply that some read more completely and carefully
than others? Are they anticipating a particular conclusion from
their reading of the entire book? Are they temperamentally prone
to focus on optimism or pessimism? Are they at times wilfully
enjoying contradicting the conclusion Forster provides?

The last chapter is very rich: glancing back; continuing echoes
of the abyss, gray, water, and grass-to-hay; advancing the story and
the characters over 14 months. Two people are left out. Jacky
presumably is in the abyss from which no traveller returns; the final
mention of the abyss is not the social one but 'the black abyss of
the past'. Tibby is not mentioned, but he had become 'moderately
a dear' (p. 291). If he was not interested in a German girl saved for

him by Frieda (p. 113), I wish Forster could have put in a line such
as 'Tibby sounded happy in his last letter from China'.

Margaret and Helen sit outdoors on a sunny afternoon as the
hay in the meadow is cut, the reaper 'encompassing with narrowing
circles the sacred centre of the field'. ('Sacred' here is worth
connecting with Henry's two uses of the word 30 pages earlier, 'I
am not one of your Bernard Shaws who consider nothing sacred',
(p. 296), a double irony, Henry apparently meaning something
quite else, yet perhaps hinting that he has qualities which can make
for his redemption. Two pages later comes the most perceptive
remark Henry ever makes: 'A house in which one has once lived
becomes in a sort of way sacred').

Tom, the six-year-old farmworker's son, is playing with Helen's
one-year-old baby, who is not named. Helen instructs 'Baby is
not to stand', which requires footnoting: rickets was believed to
be caused by babies standing too soon, before the discovery of
vitamins in 1912. Helen predicts that Tom and baby are 'going
to be lifelong friends': the yeoman to be a comrade of the
son of lower-middle-class man and upper-middle-class woman –
friendship annihilating class barriers. Margaret is now truly rural
and the seasonal cycle will 'become part of her, year after year'.
The much-loved wych-elm might threaten: 'Every westerly gale
might blow the wych-elm down and bring the end of all things.' A
Wilcox intrusion is disappearing, as they are 'sitting on the remains
of Evie's rockery'.

Helen asked in her second letter, 'Meg, shall we ever learn to
talk less?' (p. 21). Margaret now has changed: she 'was growing
less talkative'. Further, 'she never stopped working', at sewing: she
has taken on a quality she admired in Wilcoxes. 'I do not love
children', confesses Margaret: a limitation, but not a vital one with
a baby in the house: the sisters are becoming a pair, a composite
wife/mother.

'The noise of the cutter came intermittently, like the breaking
of waves', and, on the last page, 'again and again fell the word,
like the ebb of a dying sea'. This continues to the end the water
imagery (usually moving water, in flux) which began in the second
chapter with 'floodgates', the river Rhine, and Wickham Place as
a 'backwater' or 'estuary'. A man is 'preparing to scythe out' a
dell-hole and just after Margaret (whose 'eyes had been troubling
her', p. 163, on the day she became engaged to Henry) takes off

her pince-nez to watch the scything. A scythe replaces the Schlegel sword: a part of prosperous agriculture, and – carried by Father Time, the Grim Reaper – an indication of Death. (In one of the novel's more unusual ideas, taken from Michelangelo, 'Death destroys a man; the idea of Death saves him', pp. 237 and 315: thus the scythe contributes to saving).

Henry, says Margaret, is 'eternally tired', confirmed later by the narrator as 'pitiably tired'. She explains that Henry is one of 'the poeple who collapse when they do notice a thing': this changed Henry on balance has gained by learning to notice. Helen asks: 'May I tell you something? I like Henry', the consequence of change in both Henry and Helen. Helen has overcome her crippling hatred of Henry. Helen has two long speeches in which she says she will never marry, and that she is forgetting Leonard, though her eyes fill with tears as she speaks. Trilling summarises this as 'Helen confesses that she cannot love a man' (1944, p. 116) though the context is about loving Leonard. This, too, can be Helen still prone to extreme positions – though as a single mother she is not marriageable.

Margaret turns abstract, praising 'differences . . . so that there may always be colour; sorrow, perhaps, but colour in the daily gray'. ('Gray' is the commonest colour in the novel: inevitable, but to be opposed). Helen picks up 'a bunch of grass', which includes daisies and 'red and white and yellow clover', both colour and a kind of celebration of human diversity. Margaret assures her that the grass 'will sweeten tomorrow', from dead grass to hay, Life with the knowledge of Death.

The conversation turns to their life at Howards End. Helen hopes 'it will be permanant' and Margaret adds: 'There are moments when I feel Howards End peculiarly our own.' Doubt follows, for the 'red rust' of London is creeping towards the house. London previously has been gray: might a *red* London indicate improvement? Years earlier, London's 'shallows washed more widely . . . over the fields of Hertfordshire' (p. 115). (Literally, since the late 1940s, the development of Stevenage as a New Town has spread closer and closer to Forster's childhood home). Margaret, or the narrator, grows more depressed: 'The melting-pot was being prepared for them. Logically, they had no right to be alive'. Cryptically, 'were they possibly the earth beating time?' Then Margaret pins her faith on hope, not logic: 'I can't help hoping, and very early in the morning in the garden I feel that our house is the future as well as the past.'

For four and a half pages Forster has presented only the Schlegel sisters and Helen's baby. Paul Wilcox comes out of the house (the Wilcoxes having stayed indoors because of their problem of hay-fever) and reports that the Wilcoxes have been – what else – 'talking business'. Clumsy – and coarser than he was at the start – Paul kicks the front door. So 'Mrs Wilcox gave a little cry of annoyance'. This is the first time Margaret has been referred to as 'Mrs Wilcox'; she had now truly inherited her house, adopted her mysterious qualities, and added culture, intellect and the best kind of cosmopolitanism.

Henry confirms that Margaret will inherit Howards End, and after her the baby: Leonard's child will return to his great-grandparents' rural roots. Henry is giving his children money, and Margaret is gradually giving away hers – to a number of poor, aspiring Leonard Basts, perhaps. Margaret sees this as her victory: 'She, who had never expected to conquer anyone, had charged straight through these Wilcoxes and broken up their lives' – not connection, but conquest. As Paul, Evie and Dolly leave Howards End, Dolly lets slip that the first Mrs Wilcox intended Margaret to have the house.

After Margaret has laid her head in Henry's hands (submissive, or happily-married couple?), she asks what Dolly meant, and Henry answers that he 'went into it thoroughly' and found it 'clearly fanciful', which is rather less than half the truth and casts doubt on the kind of man Henry has become. 'Margaret was silent', no longer a facile talker but with new profound wisdom. 'Something shook [Margaret's] life in its inmost recesses, and she shivered', some intimation, perhaps, that she must either confront Henry for the second time in their lives, or let the moment pass. She chooses to bypass the problem: 'Nothing has been done wrong.'

Kenneth Graham is very disturbed by this:

> If Margaret's inward shudder is not to be taken as a frisson of that dying sea, an ebbing of her new security at this reminder of unassuageable betrayals, and is no more than a shiver of fearful pleasure at seeing how Mrs Wilcox's wishes have come right in the end, then her 'Nothing has been done wrong' is an egregious self-betrayal and self-delusion. And on the other hand

if her 'Nothing has been done wrong' is a tragically conscious
gesture of ironic pacification towards the Wilcox crassness, then
her shudder is indeed an echo of that momentary cosmic sense
of disaster and chaos. Either way . . . it is a deathly note to strike
amid the celebration of new life, Helen's baby, and the joy
of harvest . . . It is . . . one of those moments where a totally
different register suddenly declares itself within the bland or
witty cadences of his prose, jolts our attention to a quite
different line of thought or feeling, and casts a new light of
suggestiveness on everything that has gone before, hinting at
contradictory combinations or ramifying echoes in the text that
has been already unfolded.   (1988, pp. 157–8)

Norman Page offers two possible interpretations: 'Unless we read
this as a reassurance to a half-senile man rather than a meaningful
statement, it may be taken as implying a disturbing shift in the
firm moral stance that Margatet has maintained throughout the
book; and some have interpreted it as Forster's recognition that
real life calls for compromises than may amount to a betrayal of
liberal ideas. Equally, though, it can be taken as expressing a faith
in meliorism – in the gradual betterment of the human condition
and the inevitable victory of right' (1977, p. 94).

Judith Weissman defends the words as a vision: 'Nothing has been
done wrong because a divinity has been using the Wilcoxes and
the Schlegels for her own ends, bringing them back to an ancient
agricultural life, not as the fanciful choice of dilettantes, but as an
economic and moral necessity' (1987, p. 282).

Helen rushes into the house, with laughter, excitement and
'infectious joy', shouting 'The field's cut! We've seen to the very
end, and it'll be such a crop of hay as never!' Affirmative, yet
'never' is an ominous word, and a word is missing: such a crop
of hay as never *before* or as never *again?*

The three classes, Schlegel, Wilcox and Bast, are now mixed, and
the child is with a fourth class, the son of a yeoman, the class which
is 'England's hope' (p. 314). The child will inherit the Schlegels'
furniture in Howards End, connecting town and country. Helen
has a new acceptance of Nature. The meadow will go on producing
hay – and Wilcoxes will go on having hay-fever. The ramparts resist
the goblins. Howards End has become a female house, with the
eventual owner a male.

The novel ends in splendour in the present, in sunshine on harvest home. This is 'the peace of the country . . . the peace of the present, which passes understanding' (p. 307). The world still contains Wilcoxian materialism; urban blight; the modern craze for movement, for more and faster cars.

Not only these, World War I was approaching, and Rose Macaulay, in the first book about Forster of 1938, sees *Howards End* as essentially pre-1914; standing 'as a delicate and exquisitely wrought monument to an age when liberty, equality, and fraternity were not absurd cries, when the world was not in so perilously catastrophic a state that to pursue art, grace, elegance and wit savoured of lack of public spirit, when culture was something other to writers than the negation of Fascism, and intellectual liberty was a personal rather than a political aim' (1938, pp. 126–7).

Forster ended *A Room with a View* with the conventional happy ending of a marriage and ended *A Passage to India* with 'No, not now; no, not there'. In *Howards End* he is less clear-cut with people, closing in what Anne Wright calls 'non-discursive modernist prose or indeed poetry' (1984, p. 62). John Edward Hardy rightly identifies 'a fertility ritual': '"Circles"', a '"sacred centre"', baby, bumper crop. The transcendent extrapersonalist principle to which Forster makes his final appeal is, purely and simply, the fertility principle . . . The house endures. But there is one thing still longer enduring – namely, the land itself. And it is there, in the field, that the drama of human survival finds its valid and final, "sacred centre"' (1964, pp. 48, 50). William Thickstun's phrase, 'visionary closure', in his book of that name adds an acceptance of what Forster achieves in the last chapter, and associates the novel with other twentieth century texts, such as *The Rainbow*, where the end is pure vision. (Forster believed in the need for a 'rainbow bridge' to 'connect the prose in us with the passion', casually dropping in his rainbow allusion halfway through, p. 187).

The merit, suggests Peter Widdowson, is in the absence of a clear-cut resolution: 'It is precisely in the tensions, irresolutions and ambiguities of the novel that its strength resides' (1977, p. 12). More helpful is Alan Friedman's view, that Forster intends to avoid finality in his conclusions: 'His endings lead his characters (and his readers) invariably outward: at the end he sets their lives (readers' and characters') into motion rather than at rest' (1972, p. 431).

This intriguing aspect is taken further by Frederick Karl and Marvin Magalaner: 'To Margaret and Helen, as to Mrs Wilcox before them, falls the power to make what they will of Howards End and of England. It is not clear to Forster or to the reader whether they will succeed' (1959, p. 119).

Forster had expressed this aim himself in *Aspects of the Novel*: 'Expansion. That is the idea the novelist must cling to. Not completion. Not rounding off but opening out. When the symphony is over we feel that the notes and tunes composing it have been liberated, they have found in the rhythm of the whole their individual freedom. Cannot the novel be like that?' (pp. 149–50). Hence Forster ends by saying both that rural peace and stability is possible and that flux is with us – though no river or tide can wash away the wych-elm.

Part 2
Appraisal

1 Aspects of the Style

'Only connect' is practised throughout the novel. The recurrence of such phrases as 'see life steadily and see it whole', 'telegrams and anger' and 'panic and emptiness' are conspicuous even at first reading, perhaps also 'hands on the ropes' and others. Some of the connections are light: Howards End is a rabbit warren (p. 21); Helen thinks Mrs Wilcox carries hay for rabbits (p. 20); Leonard entering his street glances 'like a rabbit that is going to bolt into its hole' (p. 59); clerks in Wilcox's office are in rabbit-hutches (p. 196); Wilcoxes breed like rabbits (p. 269); the boy at Howards End thinks Tibby is the name of a rabbit (p. 293). Leonard cuts his finger on the broken glass of a photograph frame (pp. 60–1) and soon after Margaret does the same (p. 82), which links the subjects of the photos, Jacky and Dolly. Glass is also associated with Mrs Wilcox vanishing behind the glass doors of a lift (p. 95), 'the long glass saloon' of the train to Oniton (p. 209) and 'the glass shade . . . that cuts off married couples from the world' (p. 254). There are dozens more, repeated and varied: umbrellas, hats and top-hats, swords and soldiers, ghosts, books, gray, the moon and adventures, dust and the abyss, talking and not talking, mysteries, muddles and mistakes (Mrs Moore in *A Passage to India* liked mysteries and hated muddles). Some of these are verbal play, some serve to link one group of characters with another or one place with another, others are minor symbols. All these provide rhythm in the novel.

Grass, and grass becoming hay, provides one of the two major rhythmic devices. E. K. Brown identified this in his pioneering *Rhythm in the Novel* in 1950:

> The sequence of the wisps of hay, the bunch of weeds, the trickling grass, the grass on the Six Hills, the bumper crop of

> hay [20, 36, 200, 245, 324, Chap. 44], is not the only symbol
> for the life that is immune to Wilcoxism . . . The hay is linked
> with everything that stands out against Wilcoxism: with the
> countryside and the past; with Margaret's cultivation of personal
> relations; with Helen's reckless revolt against the empire of
> business and convention; and, in the scarcely individuated
> baby, with a junction of the poor, the urban poor who have
> rural roots, and those generous elements in other classes which,
> if dependent on big business, are not defiled, depersonalized
> by it. Above all these describable things stands, as presiding
> goddess, Ruth Howard, in whom there is something that no
> description can exhaust, any more than it can exhaust the hay
> itself.   (pp. 50–1)

Moreover, the Wilcoxes – and Tibby – all suffer from hay-fever, and
hay is literally a part of the English rural scene.

George H. Thomson is more precise about the symbolism here,
recalling 'Death destroys a man; the idea of Death saves him'
(pp. 237, 315): 'Grass because it is alive is subject to destruction,
it is in a state of dying; whereas hay, once it has withered and
sweetened, has passed beyond destruction and has a new and
permanent value, it is in a state of living.' He builds a parallel:
'Wickham Place [which is demolished] is to Howards End as grass
is to hay' (1967, pp. 186–7).

An even more important image is water, particularly moving
water, since this contrasts with the immobility and near-
timelessness of Howards End. Though Howards End survives and
continues, London is rather oddly associated with water, 'bricks
and mortar rising and falling with the restlessness of the water in
a fountain' (p. 59). James McConkey in 1957 identified 'the master
image of the whole novel [is] that of water, of rivers and the sea: for
water may represent not only continuity and the "deeper stream"
and man's merging with the infinite; it may represent . . . quite the
opposite, flux without meaning or purpose, and man may be lost
on the sea, a wanderer exiled from peace and from home' (p. 123).
John S. Martin placed the effect: 'Connecting the known with the
unknown, the sea symbolizes the universe, formless, illimitable,
and challenging, in which man must try to chart a course' (1976,
p. 118). Kenneth Graham is much more exact, finding opposites
which can never connect: the sea 'is simultaneously (like the realm

of spirit and mystery) a great authority and (like the realm of business mores, panic, and emptiness) a force of erosion and hopeless flux' (1988, p. 173).

Water is often a metaphor associated with characters: Henry advises of Leonard, 'Let him leave the ship before it sinks' (p. 140) and Henry is soon 'out of my depth' (p. 159). Of Margaret, after the death of Mrs Wilcox: 'Paul and his mother, ripple and great wave, had flowed into her life and ebbed out of it for ever. The ripple had left no traces behind; the wave had strewn at her feet fragments torn from the unknown. A curious seeker, she stood for a while at the verge of the sea that tells so little, but tells a little, and watched the outgoing of this last tremendous tide' (p. 110). Similarly, when Helen is 'stranded' with the Basts for the night at Oniton, 'now that the wave of excitement was ebbing . . . she asked herself what forces had made the wave flow' (p. 231).

The rivers are actual ones: a little river runs on three sides of the mansion at Oniton (p. 214) and the Frome, Stour and Avon can be seen from the Purbeck Hills (p. 170). The river Thames separates Leonard in south London from Schlegels and Wilcoxes north of the river, though Leonard does not look at the Thames as he walks over Westminster Bridge (p. 59), perhaps to delay connecting him with water until Helen 'baptises' him as he lies dead. The gulf between Schlegel and Wilcox is shown when they react differently watching the tide crest on Chelsea Embankment (pp. 135–43).

Dust, rabbits and the like provide a kind of rhythm; grass/hay and many forms of water provide rhythm-and-symbol; Howards End, the wych-elm and others provide symbols. Thomson has a neat formulation: 'The hay symbolizes individual life; the house, individual life in relation to family, that is to ancestors and heirs; the wych-elm, individual life in relation to the total life of man rooted in an unknown past and branching into an unknown future. The word *life* is prominent in these formulations. But death is everywhere implicit' (1967, p. 174). This is too neat. The house and tree connect tradition, the past, the earth, beauty, Englishness. Grass and hay add life, death and the Knowledge of Death. Mrs Wilcox, the meadow, the vine and the Six Hills are also a part of the pattern, a pattern of true symbolism, of deliberate imprecision.

As the time-scheme of the novel appears never to have been set out, it is sketched here, presuming the end to be in the present, the year of publication:

Spring 1905	Margaret and Helen Schlegel meet Henry and Ruth Wilcox in Germany
June 1905	Helen stays at Howards End
11 November 1905	Charles marries Dolly
December 1905	Mrs Wilcox dies, before Christmas
March-April 1908	'over two years passed', p. 115; Tibby 'was down for the Easter vacation', p. 117. Rapid sequence of events: Jacky and Leonard visit Schlegels; Henry meets Schlegels on Chelsea Embankment.
August 1908	Evie marries Percy Cahill at Oniton
September 1908	Margaret marries Henry
April 1909	Helen goes to Howards End; Margaret's defiance of Henry; killing of Leonard
June 1910	'Fourteen months had passed', p. 325: final chapter.

Oliver Stallybrass is impatient with Forster's casualness about chronology, footnoting that 'Leonard's turn of phrase ... show a vagueness about chronology which argues an equal degree of vagueness in his creator' (p. 348). Dolly does have rather a lot of babies rather quickly (pp. 187, 199) and the delays caused by Easter traffic (p. 198) come long after Tibby's return to Wickham Place for the Easter vacation.

2   The Good

Forster's ideas, examined here and in the next section, are sometimes personal and original, sometimes familiar, sometimes apparently banal but given a new spin. Other ideas are revealing of the time and place, Edwardian England. The fictional form combines, juxtaposes and diffuses these ideas.

i   *Howards End and the Wych-Elm*
Howards End itself is almost a character in the book.
(J. K. Johnstone, 1954, p. 223)

[Howards End] constitutes a civilisation and shapes character.   (Christopher Gillie, 1983, p. 118).

The house (the home of traditional wisdom), the wych elm
(superstition on its way to faith) and the meadow (the beauty,
joy and dignity of labour) are his attempt to embody [religious
feelings].   (R. N. Parkinson, 1979, p. 68)

Helen at the start puts 'Howards End' as the place she writes
from and introduces the house to her sister as 'old and little, and
altogether delightful', continuing: 'There's a very big wych-elm – to
the left as you look up – leaning a little over the house, and standing
on the boundary between the garden and meadow. I quite love that
tree already' (p. 19). The story begins and ends at Howards End.
Henry eventually explains some of the history, in his eyes, a story of
mortgages and mismanagement (p. 205). He finds it 'picturesque
enough, but not a place to live in . . . We feel that it is neither one
thing nor the other' (pp. 141, 142). Later, perhaps influenced by
Margaret, he sees more: 'A house in which one has once lived
becomes in a sort of way sacred' (p. 298). For Mrs Wilcox it was
'a spirit' (p. 107); paradoxically, she seems to belong to the house
rather than the house to her: 'She seemed to belong not to the
young people and their motor, but to the house, and to the tree that
overshadowed it' (p. 36). As for Charles, I wouldn't touch it with
tongs myself . . . It's a measly little place' (p. 197). Margaret twice
fails to reach Howards End, first because of Tibby's illness and then
because Mrs Wilcox meets Henry and Evie at the railway station.
Margaret is finally able to go in alone in Chapter 23 (pp. 200–2)
when she senses 'the heart of the house beating, faintly at first,
then loudly, martially'. Howards End is only a resting place for
Wilcoxes; Mr Bryce, the tenant, leaves after a few weeks; Leonard
is fitted to attain it, but not to stay there; Charles at the end will
not live anywhere near it; only Margaret and Helen, though first
using it as a furniture warehouse, are truly fitted to possess it. Helen
in fact speaks 'as if the garden was also part of their childhood'
(p. 291), while Margaret comes to love England through the house
and through Miss Avery (p. 205).
     Leonard and Jacky Bast become homeless, and Leonard refuses
to take an interest in his roots. The Wilcoxes simply take on houses
as it suits them: a London flat for Charles' wedding; Ducie Street

for a while; Oniton Grange till Henry finds that it is damp and in the wrong part of Shropshire; planning to build at Midhurst in Sussex. Margaret challenges Henry: 'Don't you believe in having a permanent home?' (p. 255).

While Margaret tells Tibby 'Not to move about the world would kill me' (p. 120), Mrs Wilcox is exactly the opposite: 'Howards End was nearly pulled down once. It would have killed me' (p. 93). Wickham Place 'had helped [the Schlegels] to balance their lives, and almost to counsel them' (p. 154). It 'had always been human' and provided the Schlegels with 'thirty years of happiness' (p. 253). (Thirty years connects Schlegels and Wilcoxes, who experienced thirty years of marriage, p. 99). Margaret is surprisingly casual about having to leave Wickham Place: 'We are fond of ours, but there is nothing distinctive about it. As you saw, it is an ordinary London house. We shall easily find another' (p. 93). Margaret even says 'I'll live anywhere', adding Swanage and seven other exceptions (p. 119). For a time Schlegels resemble Henry in a ready acceptance of flux rather than stability.

Forster's nostalgia for his childhood home (and making friends with farm boys) comes through clearly. The factual model of the house, Rooksnest, where he lived from the age of four to fourteen, on the edge of Stevenage, is confirmed by the Penguin and Abinger editions containing an appendix with Forster's essay on the house. He also writes of the house and its enormous significance for him in his biography of his great-aunt, Marianne Thornton, of 1956. A photo of the house can be found in P. N. Furbank's biography of Forster and in Wilfred Stone's critical book. The extra-textual knowledge makes the house even more important for Forster. Cavaliero comments that 'Forster's use of Rooksnest . . . is a perfect example of that mythologising of his private life which makes him as a novelist so intimate and yet portentous' (1979, p. 107). Readers who may not be able to create an English house imaginatively may enjoy Rosalind Ashe's dainty, pretty version in her *Literary Houses: 10 Famous Houses in Fiction* (London, 1982, pp. 116–25) – the kind of book which does not find its way into university libraries!

The meaning of the house is clearest in an explicit passage deleted in the manuscript: 'That is the importance of Howards End, or of any scene that the reader may hold dear. It is poetry, while London is culture. It is not a movement, for it rests on the earth' (*The Manuscripts of 'Howards End'*, 1973, p. 275). 'Starting from Howards End, [Margaret] attempted to realize England' (p. 204) – in fact, the house is the best of England. Howards End finally is enriched not only by the presence of the Schlegel sisters but with their furniture and books, moved from London but some surely connected with their father's previous homes in Manchester and Germany. Though Howards End changes Margaret and Helen, Howards End too is changed from rural farmhouse by this addition of cosmopolitanism.

With the Wilcoxes in possession, the house was 'irrevocably masculine' (p. 56) except for the drawing-room which men had clumsily attempted to make nice for ladies (p. 290). Rightly perceived, 'house and tree transcended any simile of sex' (p. 206). Howards End brings together beauty, permanence, tradition, stability, the past, the country, a healthy way of life.

Mrs Wilcox is the human who has absorbed all that is best of the house. She is first seen by Helen, in her garden in the early morning, smelling flowers and carrying hay. She adds that Mrs Wilcox 'is sweeter than ever, and I never saw anything like her steady unselfishness' (pp. 20–1). Next she separates Helen and Paul, and Charles and Aunt Juley, rightly and decisively. Margaret perceives her thus: 'She was not intellectual, nor even alert, and it was odd that, all the same, she should give the idea of greatness . . . There was no bitterness in Mrs Wilcox; there was not even criticism; she was lovable, and no ungracious or uncharitable word had passed her lips' (p. 86). This is of the unwell Mrs Wilcox, in uncongenial London. Her chief object is ensuring the survival of Howards End: she had saved the vine but been browbeaten into allowing the building of a garage on the paddock (p. 102). She moves quietly in a world of telegrams and anger, of newspapers and motor-cars and golf-clubs, and is unaffected by them. She has an inner life and has no need to strive for this; she sees life whole. She 'knew no more of worldly wickedness and wisdom than did the flowers in her garden, or the grass in her field' (p. 99) – meaning that she knew a great deal about these? Margaret learns to distinguish 'knowledge such as hers [and] knowledge such as mine' (p. 306). She has wisdom from tradition, the past and the country.

After her death, she reappears to supervise Henry proposing marriage to Margaret: 'Mrs Wilcox strayed in and out, ever a welcome ghost; surveying the scene, thought Margaret, without one hint of bitterness' (p. 170).

She is a human being, but of an exceptional kind, when first explained: 'She seemed to belong not to the young people and their motor, but to the house, and to the tree that overshadowed it. One knew that she worshipped the past, and that the instinctive wisdom the past can alone bestow had descended upon her – that wisdom to which we give the clumsy name of aristocracy. High-born she might not be. But assuredly she cared about her ancestors, and let them help her' (p. 36). (Cavaliero is irritated by 'one knew' because 'it induces the sense of a profered superiority', 1979, p. 112). Mrs Wilcox is an aristocrat in feeling, not breeding. Forster's essay of 1939, 'What I Believe', develops the idea: 'I believe in aristocracy, though – if that is the right word, and if a democrat may use it. Not an aristocracy of power, based upon rank and influence, but an aristocracy of the sensitive, the considerate and the plucky. Its members are to be found in all nations and classes, and all through the ages, and there is a secret understanding between them when they meet. They represent the true human tradition, the one permanent victory of our queer race over cruelty and chaos ... They are sensitive for others as well as for themselves, they are considerate without being fussy, their pluck is not swankiness but the power to endure, and they can take a joke' (*Two Cheers for Democracy*, 1965, p. 81). Sensitive and considerate are certainly apposite, while 'plucky' at first is out of place, though Forster enjoys using a dated or colloquial term. Dying, she resembles a saint, because 'the light of the fire, the light from the window, and the light of a candle-lamp, which threw a quivering halo round her hands, combined to create a strange atmosphere of dissolution' (p. 78). Mrs Wilcox has to carry most significance near the end, when Margaret speaks to Helen: 'I feel that you and I and Henry are only fragments of that woman's mind. She knows everything. She is everything. She is the house, and the tree that leans over it' (p. 305).

This is an extraordinary weight for even an extraordinary woman to bear, yet she convinces as a character in the novel. Robert Langbaum comments: 'She is the most memorable character in *Howards End*, for she carries her own atmosphere with her; she is not just another character, she is another order of existence altogether' (1970, p. 137). Lionel Trilling is impressed: 'As a character Ruth Wilcox is remarkably – and perhaps surprisingly – successful. Her "reality" is of a strange kind and consists in her having no reality in the ordinary sense – she does not have, that is, the reality of personality, of idiosyncracy or even of power. Her strength comes exactly from her lack of force, her distinction from her lack of distinguishing traits. She suggests Shakespeare's "gentle" women, the Countess of *All's Well* (1944, p. 104). Judith Weissman instead puts the emphasis on her representing 'a real and good possible life, a genuine basis for an economy, and a radical hope for England' (1987, p. 277).

Mrs Wilcox, though a good and dutiful wife and mother, is connected more deeply to the house and to the past. She has only three scenes of connecting to Margaret, and all in London, away from her home. The first is Margaret's visit to her to apologize for a thoughtless letter, and although Margaret is 'startled and a little annoyed' by Mrs Wilcox's enigmatic remark, 'I almost think you forget you're a girl' (p. 83), rapport is established. The lunch-party is the second, and here other guests prevent real contact until Mrs Wilcox is leaving; then they shake hands 'with a newborn emotion' (p. 88). The third is nearly as unsatisfactory, Christmas shopping in the fog, and only at the end is there a chance to connect – the invitation to Howards End which Margaret declines (Ch. 10). Margaret is too talkative: what Mrs Wilcox can teach her is not verbal. Margaret becomes Mrs Wilcox after Leonard's death (and surely when she is permanently living in Howards End) in the most cryptic passage in the novel: 'Life was a deep, deep river, death a blue sky, life was a house, death a wisp of hay, a flower, a tower, life and death were anything and everything, except this ordered insanity . . . There were truer relationships beyond the limits that fetter us now' (p. 320).

The Schlegels' father also continues his influence after his death. His sword is preserved; his books must be kept, if not read; his ideas have shaped the thinking of his children. The loss of the London house matters because it breaks a link with him. 'Was father alive?', asks Margaret as they reminisce about furniture in Howards End (p. 291). The seen, the furniture, links them to the unseen, the past.

Miss Avery, who continues the spirit of Mrs Wilcox, is 'no maundering old woman. Her wrinkles were shrewd and humorous. She looked capable of scathing wit and also of high but unostentatious nobility', thinks Margaret (p. 267). She has lived near Howards End for so long that she knows everything: the house speaks to her. She is the keeper of the keys, and takes on the 'guardianship' of the Schlegels' furniture (p. 253). She is 'invisible' in Howards End (p. 265) and knows when Madge is thinking about hats (pp. 263, 265), like Mrs Wilcox's immediate grasp of the Helen/Paul situation.

Miss Avery connects both Mrs Wilcox and the house to Margaret. She arranges the Schlegels' furniture in the house, and points mysteriously to Margaret inheriting the spirit of the woman:

> 'I took you for Ruth Wilcox.'
> Margaret stammered: 'I – Mrs Wilcox – I?'
> 'In fancy, of course' (p. 202).

Miss Avery sets up the closing events. She has planned for the milk to be sent, which gives Margaret and Helen the idea of staying the night, which is the reason for Margaret defying Henry; for Charles being in the house when Leonard arrives; and for the sword hanging there when Charles wants to hit Leonard. Miss Avery is a Wise Woman, like Mrs Wilcox, a living link to the past, with a prophetic gift.

That the house gives roots to those who appreciate it provides a link to the wych-elm, 'an English tree. No report had prepared [Margaret] for its peculiar glory. It was neither warrior, nor lover, nor god; in none of these roles do the English excel. It was a comrade, bending over the house, strength and adventure in its roots, but in its utmost fingers tenderness, and the girth, that a dozen men could not have spanned, became in the end evanescent, till pale bud clusters seemed to float in the air' (p. 206). Even Henry values it: 'I shouldn't want that fine wych-elm spoiled' (p. 190). Helen and Paul kiss 'under the column of the vast wych-elm' (p. 39); Helen and Margaret are truly re-united beside it (Ch. 39).

The reader's eye is taken over the surface of the tree, from its huge base to the barely visible tips of the branches. The deeper connections are with the house and the earth, and with the air, the sun and the moon. The roots of the tree explore the soil and feed from its nutrients, becoming a part of the earth of England – as does Mrs Wilcox, buried nearby, who 'lay under the earth now' (p. 99).

The meadow and the encumbering, unprolific vine add to the picture, as do the Six Hills, 'tombs of warriors, breasts of the spring' (p. 301), at the other end of the village of Hilton.

ii England

[*Howards End*] asks the question, 'Who shall inherit England?'   (Lionel Trilling, 1944, p. 102)

England becomes a character and its health is a central subject.   (Daniel R. Schwarz, 1989, p. 127)

Behind the rather cozy domesticity of *Howards End* lies a full-scale attempt on Forster's part to create an English myth.   (Elizabeth Barrett, 1982, p. 155).

Howards End is often described as a Condition of England novel, a 19th century form associated with Thomas Carlyle and such novels as Mrs Gaskell's *North and South*. The phrase took on a new life in 1909 when C. F. G. Masterman published a study entitled *The Condition of England*. His idealism and humane values influenced such novels as H. G. Wells' *Tono-Bungay* and Ford Madox Ford's *The Good Soldier*. Masterman gave writers a reason to attempt to engage with all of England, with the fundamental problems of the age. Margaret Drabble has continued this convention in the 1980s.

Leonard ('I'm an Englishman', p. 65) and Henry (thinking of his adultery with Jacky, 'he was a good average Englishman, who had slipped', p. 243) assert their Englishness. Aunt Juley asserts in Chapter 2: 'I regard you Schlegels as English, English to the backbone' (p. 23), and soon after the narrator explains that they are half-German (p. 42). Henry thinks Simpson's in the Strand (still there in 1992, 150 years old, its identity unchanged) 'so thoroughly Old English' (p. 156); Margaret knows the restaurant is 'no more Old English than the works of Kipling' (p. 157). Margaret at Howards End 'attempted to realize England' (p. 204); Wilcoxes 'keep England going' (p. 268), says Margaret, the loyal fianceé, to Miss Avery; yet she only grows fond of England after marrying Henry (p. 306).

Such comments, by and about characters, keep the subject of England before us. So does Chapter 19: 'If one wanted to show a foreigner England, perhaps the wisest course whould be to take him to the final section of the Purbeck hills . . . [The Isle of Wight] is as if a fragment of England floated forward to greet the foreigner . . . The imagination swells, spreads and deepens, until it becomes geographic and encircles England.' The view includes countryside, rivers, coast, suburbia and 'the City's trail'. The tide ebbs and flows, reflecting the mind of Margaret as she considers marrying Henry. In case the passage is too high-flown, the tone is deflated by English-German bickering between Frieda and Aunt Juley. At the end of the chapter, 'England was alive', and three questions follow, the most important about ownership, 'Does she belong to those who have moulded her?' Wilcoxes. Or to those with vision, who 'have somehow seen her' (p. 175), Schlegels?

The Purbeck Hills are reached from Aunt Juley's Swanage, ugly, growing, with 'mincing waves' (p. 161) which beat the 'gentlest of tattoos upon the sand' (p. 270).

Swanage, the seaside resort, is contrasted with two counties, Hertfordshire and Shropshire. All three are reached by train from London, but Henry finds Shropshire 'too far from London' (p. 256) which can protect it. Forster carefully defines the differing beauties of the counties: beauty which can only be appreciated by standing and staring, not properly seen from a moving car or train. 'Hertfordshire is England at its quietest, with little emphasis of river and hill; it is England meditative' (p. 198), while 'Shropshire had not the reticence of Hertfordshire' (p. 210). Shropshire resembles the wild, near-classless Wiltshire of *The Longest Journey* while Hertfordshire is like the Home Counties of *A Room with a View*. Hilton and Oniton both have a house near a church and a village, but Oniton 'had for ages served that lonely valley, and guarded our marches against the Celt' (p. 208). Oniton adjoins Wales, and old enmities can be connected by Margaret: 'Saxon or Celt? But it doesn't matter. Whichever you are, you will have to listen to me' (p. 216). Unfortunate urban Leonard succeeds in visiting Surrey, Shropshire and finally Hertfordshire.

Oniton looks west to the mysterious, unspoiled Welsh mountains. At Hilton station, on the other hand, one wonders 'into which country will it lead, England or Suburbia?' (pp. 29–30). Margaret has the answer, walking from the station to Howards End: 'The appearance of the land was neither aristocratic nor suburban' (p. 263).

The rest of the country is brought in through an early paragraph about London railway stations: 'In Paddington all Cornwall is latent and the remoter west; down the inclines of Liverpool Street lie fenlands and the illimitable Broads; Scotland is through the pylons of Euston; Wessex behind the poised chaos of Waterloo' (p. 27). Norfolk and Sussex enter as places where Henry may build houses; Lincolnshire as the home of most of Leonard's ancestors; Lancashire is the home of the Schlegels' mother and Yorkshire is where Henry and Evie go motoring. Leonard walks south from Wimbledon into the Surrey woods, passing close to Epsom, where Charles used to live. Oxford may have only a faint 'claim to represent England', but – unlike London and Swanage – shows that a town can be beautiful (this is Oxford before Morris Motors!) 'The lovely creature raised domes and spires into the cloudless blue' (p. 251). Shrewsbury, too, is an 'astonishing city' (p. 210).

As for London, the novel traces both Margaret and Forster turning against the city. When Mrs Wilcox remarks that 'there is nothing to get up for in London', culture-vulture Margaret is 'scandalized': 'When there are all the autumn exhibitions, and Ysaye playing in the afternoon! Not to mention people' (p. 80). When Margaret responds to the Oniton landscape in the dusk, she has changed to 'I hate London' (p. 216). Seeing London through the eyes of Mrs Wilcox, Christmas shopping in the fog, London becomes Hell: 'The city seemed satanic, the narrower streets oppressing like the galleries of a mine' (p. 94). Soon after, the novelist pauses and allows himself an essay: 'To speak against London is no longer fashionable. The earth as an artistic cult has had its day, and the literature of the near future will probably ignore the country and seek inspiration from the town . . . Certainly London fascinates. One visualizes it as a tract of quivering gray, intelligent without purpose' (p. 116).

This leads to explaining Margaret's newfound dislike of the city, the loss of her house: 'The Londoner seldom understands his city until it sweeps him, too, away from his moorings, and Margaret's eyes were not opened until the lease of Wickham Place expired . . . In the streets of the city she noted for the first time the architecture of hurry, and heard the language of hurry on the mouths of its inhabitants . . . Month by month things were stepping livelier, but to what goal?' (p. 116).

The key charge against London is its fluidity, its constant changing. The narrator voices the point: 'The city herself . . . rose and fell in a continual flux . . . This famous building had arisen, that was doomed. Today Whitehall had been transformed: it would be the turn of Regent Street tomorrow' (p. 115). Margaret has the same insight later: 'I hate this continual flux of London. It is an epitome of us at our worst – eternal formlessness; all the qualities, good, bad and indifferent, streaming away – streaming, streaming for ever. That's why I dread it so' (p. 184). Margaret's epiphany about London comes when Tibby wonders if Helen suffers from mental illness: 'The mask fell off the city, and she saw it for what it really is – a caricature of infinity.' She goes into St Paul's cathedral, yet even here she found flux, not stability: The dome of St Paul's 'stands out of the welter so bravely, as if preaching the gospel of form. But, within, St Paul's is as its surroundings – echoes and whispers, inaudible songs, invisible mosaics, wet footmarks crossing and recrossing the floor. *Si monumentum requiris, circumspice*: it points us back to London' (pp. 274–5). J. B. Beer rightly sees this as 'a low point in the novel', probably the lowest, and a 'moment of horror' (1962, p. 113). Leonard glimpses Margaret at this time (p. 310); people not connecting for a moment suggests Leopold and Stephen wandering in Dublin separately in Joyce's *Ulysses*. Both *Ulysses* and *Howards End* (together with George Gissing's London and Arnold Bennett's Five Towns) suggest the novel growing more urban and novelists adopting attitudes to this urbanisation.

John Colmer writes:

Howards End is not only a powerful 'Condition of England' novel; it is also a novel about the modern city. Throughout *Howards End*, Forster builds up a powerful contrast between the slow natural rhythms of the earth associated with Mrs Wilcox's house, Howards End, and the hectic pace of life in London, as more and more people are crammed onto its soil and the anonymous forces of modern capitalism transform the city into a gigantic emblem of human muddle . . . while the image of London in *Howards End* lacks the cosmic terror of the image of the Marabar Caves in *A Passage to India*, it nevertheless renders in a most disturbing manner all those forces in modern civilisation that defy the liberal imagination's power to create visions of order and harmony out of urban chaos.   (Colmer, 1978, pp. 154–5).

London in fact is fragmenting, artificial, spreading: the negativity of T. S. Eliot's 'Waste Land' is anticipated.

Forster himself, in a relaxed essay in 1937, entitled 'London is a Muddle', likes the city better than before: 'Though it is not practicable to love such a place (one could as easily embrace both volumes of the Telephone Directory at once), one can love bits of it and become interested in the rest' (*Two Cheers for Democracy*, 1965, p. 359).

London is condemned as too big and too unstable, Swanage is ugly, and suburbia threatens. Further, Forster's England is south of a line from Shropshire to Hertfordshire and thus excludes almost all industrial England. The England Forster idolizes and eulogizes is far from England as it is: he offers a vision of a sunny, classless and wholly rural nation.

Wales enters the novel only as a mountainous and mysterious West, home of Celts, so Welsh and Scots readers may feel non-persons. Forster is identifying Englishness rather than Britishness, and finds England alone almost too large to comprehend.

The Schlegels connect England and Germany. Like the King of the time, Edward VII, they have a German father. They keep alive the best part of German culture, of 'mild intellectual light' (p. 43), despite change in Germany. Helen escapes when Paul is in the flat opposite Wickham Place by going to Germany, and escapes there again after her night with Leonard; her plan is to join Monica in Munich to raise her baby. The Schlegels at the start are cosmopolitan in the best sense, and by the end this quality enables them to express the best of Englishness.

Margaret and Henry honeymoon in Innsbruck in Austria and Charles and Dolly in Naples, where Helen thinks of spending the winter of her pregnancy. Italy is unattainable for Leonard, so he reads John Ruskin on Venice. Henry has made business visits to Greece and Cyprus. The world beyond Europe is touched on: Henry's company deals in West African rubber; Paul works in Nigeria; Charles fought in the Boer War; Dolly's people are Indian Army; Tibby considers becoming a Chinese interpreter; British policy to Tibet is mentioned; Mrs Warrington, a wedding guest at Oniton, has completed a 'tour round the world' (p. 207). Forster has written a novel of England and of London, dropping in a few references as reminders of England as one part of planet Earth.

iii   Beethoven

The section of the novel about Beethoven's Fifth Symphony is perhaps equivalent to the section about the Marabar caves in *A Passage to India*, but instead of 'Oum-boum' this time the message is positive.

The thinking of Forster and the Bloomsbury Group is often shown as derived from the Cambridge philosopher G. E. Moore and particularly his *Principia Ethica*, published in 1903. While Forster may not have read this, he certainly moved in circles which had accepted Moore's views. Moore uses the symphony as an example:

> The presence of some emotion is necessary to give any very high value to a state of aesthetic appreciation . . . What value should we attribute to the proper emotion excited by hearing Beethoven's Fifth Symphony, if that emotion were entirely unaccompanied by any consciousness, either of the notes, or of the melodic and harmonic relations between them? And that the mere hearing of the Symphony, even accompanied by the appropriate emotion, is not sufficient, may be easily seen, if we consider what would be the state of a man, who should hear all the notes, but should not be aware of any of those melodic and harmonic relations, which are necessary to constitute the smallest beautiful elements in the Symphony.   (pp. 190, 192)

When Forster himself writes about music, he is as so often casual and disarming. An essay of 1939 illuminates the chapter in *Howards End*:

> Listening to music is such a muddle that one scarcely knows how to start describing it. The first point to get clear in my own case is that during the greater part of every performance I do not attend. The nice sounds make me think of something else . . . What do I hear during the intervals when I do attend? Two sorts of music. They melt into each other all the time, and are not easy to christen, but I will call one of them 'music that reminds me of something', and the other 'music itself'. I used to be very fond of music that reminded me of something . . . I thought that music must be the better for having a meaning. I think so still, but am less clear as to what 'a meaning' is . . . When

music reminded me of something else that was not music, I supposed it was getting me somewhere. 'How like Monet!' I thought when listening to Debussy, and 'how like Debussy!' when looking at Monet. I translated sounds into colours, saw the piccolo as apple-green, and the trumpets as scarlet. The arts were to be enriched by taking in one another's washing . . .

The sounds! It is for them that we come, and the closer we can get up against them the better. So I do prefer 'music itself' and listen to it and for it as far as possible . . . Music is so very queer that an amateur is bound to get muddled when writing about it. It seems to be more 'real' than anything, and to survive when the rest of civilization decays . . . There's an insistence in music – expressed largely through rhythm. ('Not Listening to Music', *Two Cheers for Democracy*, pp. 133–6)

In the essay Forster writes 'sound' and in the novel 'noise': 'It will be generally admitted that Beethoven's Fifth Symphony is the most sublime noise that has ever penetrated into the ear of man . . . You are bound to admit that such a noise is cheap at two shillings' (pp. 44, 45). Glen Cavaliero probes the implications: 'How serious is that statement? It resounds; but resounding statements by Forster are always suspect and so are the people in his fiction who make them. But the use of the word 'noise' as distinct from the word 'sound' suggests an irony; and, without disrespect to a very great piece of music, one may question whether the author isn't here attempting a statement about popular taste rather than one about the music as such' (1979, p. 118).

The seven listeners hear the symphony in different ways. Helen hears goblins, who are finally scattered in a climax of 'splendour, the heroism, the youth, the magnificence of life and of death' and the 'vast roarings of superhuman joy'. Yet 'the goblins were there. They could return' (p. 47). The goblins move from Helen's consciousness to that of the narrator, and at the end of the chapter Leonard's first visit to Wickham Place is described as 'a goblin footfall' (p. 57). And on Leonard's final walk to Howards End: 'Again and again must the drums tap and the goblins stalk over the universe before joy can be purged of the superficial' (p. 315).

The account emphasises Beethoven *deciding* the direction and conclusion of his symphony: 'As if things were going too far, Beethoven took hold of the goblins and made them do what he wanted. He appeared in person . . . Beethoven chose to make all right in the end' (pp. 46, 47). The creator is not impersonal, but appears in person, and the analogy with the novelist is clear: Forster will appear from time to time and will choose to make all right in the end. Beethoven is German, and High Culture, the touchstone of sublimity in music.

Forster uses the Symphony as his example of rhythm in fiction in his *Aspects of the Novel*:

> Rhythm is sometimes quite easy. Beethoven's Fifth Symphony, for instance, starts with the rhythm 'diddidy dum', which we can all hear and tap to. But the symphony as a whole has also a rhythm – due mainly to the relation between its movements – which some people can hear but no one can tap to. The second sort of rhythm is difficult, and whether it is substantially the same as the first sort only a musician could tell us. What a literary man wants to say, though, is that the first kind of rhythm, the diddidy dum, can be found in certain novels and may give them beauty. And the other rhythm, the difficult one – the rhythm of the Fifth Symphony as a whole – I cannot quote you any parallels for that in fiction, yet it may be present.   (1974, p. 146)

The structure of the Symphony connects with the structure of the novel, certainly loosely. The pole of 'There was no such thing as splendour or heroism in the world' (p. 46) contrasts with love and poetry, just as panic and emptiness contrast with a rich inner life. 'The music had summed up to [Helen] all that had happened or could happen in her career' (p. 47), pointing to interpreting her life as successfully overcoming goblins.

J. K. Johnstone sums up: 'The effect of the structural rhythm of *Howards End* is indescribable; it is indeed comparable to the effect of a great symphony. The rhythm is so successful because it externalizes Forster's deepest emotions, his intuitions about life, and his philosophy. It is organic; not a pattern which is imposed upon the material of the novel' (1954, p. 228). Andrea Weatherhead later supplied a full demonstration of the novel paralleling the symphony, for example: 'In Beethoven's second movement, a series of variations upon a double theme takes place. The first theme is in A flat major. It is a rather smooth, flowing theme ending in a kind of cold grace. The second theme, in C major, is in a square aggressive style with a purposeful progress. One can hold closely to the themes at first, but by the end of the long movement, the extended, somewhat free plan of double variations becomes fantasizing in style . . . We see in this second movement of *Howards End* [Chaps 11 to 25] the two equivalents . . . One need not label them specifically 'inner life versus outer life', or 'country versus London', but it is fair to say that the many values in *Howards End* provide analogies to contrasts in Beethoven's symphony' (1985, pp. 254–5). If the structure of the novel is intended to echo that of the Symphony, Forster has certainly obscured it by dividing his novel only into 44 chapters.

Analogies between music and literature are difficult: David Mercer may achieve a kind of string quartet for four characters in his television drama, *Let's Murder Vivaldi* (1976). Bernard Shaw described *Heartbreak House* as 'the most musical of my plays' and when the noise of a zeppelin, dropping bombs, is heard, Hesione exclaims, 'It's splendid: it's like an orchestra: it's like Beethoven', Ellie answering 'By thunder, Hesione: it is Beethoven'. Beethoven may be the true hero of both *Heartbreak House* and *Howards End*.

3 The Ideas

'By far the most valuable things, which we know or can imagine, are certain states of consciousness, which may be roughly described as the pleasures of human intercourse and the enjoyment of beautiful objects', wrote G. E. Moore in *Principia Ethica* (1903, p. 188). These values are Bloomsbury values. The Bloomsbury Group (of Virginia Woolf, Lytton Strachey and others) has had much attention in the 1970s and 1980s, with the publication of many letters and diaries, linked with both the colourful private lives of some members and the ever-growing reputation of the novels of Woolf. Forster himself was on the edge of what was anyway a group with changing membership and loyalties, and was living outside London. Moore, concludes Michael Bell, 'turned a scepticism about general moral principles towards a pragmatic and positive approach to concrete moral situations' ('Introduction', 1980, p. 72). J. B. Priestley claims that 'Moore's heightened commonsense, scepticism, and the supreme value he attached to aesthetic enjoyments and personal relations powerfully influenced a whole remarkable group . . . The intellectual climate of Britain and America between the two World Wars would have been quite different if G. E. Moore had not published *Principia Ethica*' (1970, p. 81). The ideas promoted are the reasons for 'hope on this side of the grave' (pp. 111, 206, 320).

i. Personal Relations

Questions are important in the novel. 'Are [the Wilcoxes] our sort? Are they likely people?' (p. 23); 'Into which country will it lead, England or Suburbia?', pp. 29–30; 'How ought I to dispose of my money?', p. 132; 'For what end are [England's] fair complexities?' (p. 178) for the book's subject is answering such questions. Margaret's 'Do personal relations lead to sloppiness in the end?' (p. 41) is highly significant.

Forster's ambitious statement of 1939, 'What I Believe', asserts his own faith in personal relations:
Where do I start? With personal relationships . . . We can't know what other people are like. How, then, can we put any trust in personal relationships, or cling to them in the gathering political storm? In theory we cannot. But in practice we can and do. Though A is not unchangeably A or B unchangeably B, there can still be love and loyalty between the two. For the purpose of living one has to assume that the personality is solid, and the 'self' is an entity, and to ignore all contrary evidence. And since to ignore evidence is one of the characteristics of faith, I certainly can proclaim that I believe in personal relationships. (*Two Cheers for Democracy*, 1965, pp. 75–6)

The point is made in the abstract in the novel: 'It is private life that holds out the mirror to infinity; personal intercourse, and that alone, that ever hints at a personality beyond our daily vision' (p. 91). Personal relations, cultivated through culture, lead to a full inner life, a perception of the role of the unseen and to 'the idea of Death' (p. 236).

Young Helen gushes: 'I know that personal relations are the real life, for ever and ever' (p. 41). Though not the complete truth, she is nearer to it than Margaret when she fears sloppiness. Slightly complacent faith in personal relations leads to Helen's clumsiness with Paul at the start, to her over-valuing the Wilcoxes. Henry's contrasted indifference to the cultivating of personal relations is clearly stated: 'He was content to settle one of the greatest things in life haphazard, and so, while his investments went right, his friends generally went wrong . . . He seemed without sentiment . . . Now [Margaret] never forgot anyone for whom she had once cared' (p. 207). Henry's final collapse follows from his lack of an inner life.

Margaret's personal relations with Mrs Wilcox lead to the gift of Howards End; Helen's sexual intercourse, rather than personal intercourse, with Leonard leads to the birth of a son. Which could be sloppiness, yet assures the inheritance of Howards End.

A shared faith in personal relations, and lifelong cultivation of them, twice resolves difficulties between Margaret and Helen. First, when Helen is shocked that Margaret is going to marry Henry: 'Their inner life was so safe that they could bargain over externals . . . There are moments when the inner life actually "pays", when years of self-scrutiny, conducted for no ulterior motive, are suddenly of practical use. Such moments are still rare in the West; that they come at all promises a fairer future. Margaret, though unable to understand her sister, was assured against estrangement' (p. 196). Their second crisis is the reunion after Helen has been inexplicably overseas for eight months: 'Helen, still smiling, came up to her sister. She said: "It is always Meg." They looked into each other's eyes. The inner life had paid' (p. 292). (The vocabulary should be noticed here: 'pays' in inverted commas, 'paid' without. Does the Wilcoxian language of money in some way devalue what is achieved here through personal relations? Similarly, when Margaret reflects that 'Culture had worked in her own case' (p. 122), the verb chosen can cast doubt).

The final question, as John Hardy states, 'is not whether the inner life is worth sustaining – [the Schlegels] are never in any doubt on that point – but whether it can be entirely self-nourishing' (1963, p. 38). Personal relations are ultimately shown to be not quite enough. The narrator comments on the engagement of Henry and Margaret: 'If the inner life were the whole of life, their happiness had been assured' (p. 185). Schlegels need 'Wilcox energy and effectiveness' (Norman Page, 1987, p. 90). Personal relations have to take on something of the seen, of seeing life steadily. Though Schlegels know more than Wilcoxes in almost every way, they have something to learn from them. Which points to 'only connect'.

As Forster writes in 'What I Believe', personal relations are a place to start, not the complete answer. They are richly satisfying in themselves. Rightly practised, over time, they influence others. But only in the very long run can they possibly begin to solve the questions posed by Wilcoxes, Basts and the victims in the abyss.

ii   Only Connect

'Only connect' is the epigraph of the novel, though inconspicuous in small type on the Penguin title-page. The key statement comes when Margaret is anticipating marriage to Henry: 'She might yet be able to help him to the building of the rainbow bridge that should connect the prose in us with the passion. Without it we are meaningless fragments, half monks, half beasts, unconnected arches that have never joined into a man . . . Only connect! That was the whole of her sermon. Only connect the prose and the passion, and both will be exalted, and human love will be seen at its highest. Live in fragments no longer. Only connect, and the beast and the monk, robbed of the isolation that is life to either, will die' (pp. 187, 188). Typically, the passage weaves Margaret's thoughts in and out with the narrator's eloquence. Beer found it necessary to defend this: 'It is easy to see in the moralizing tone of the passage cover for an absence of thought: that is what we are nowadays encouraged to see in moralizing tones . . . There is in fact a degree of exact thought within the heightened style' (1962, p. 122). Surely only a jaded and oversophisticated reader is going to deny the thought here.

Connecting, we read later, requires proportion: 'The businessman who assumes that this life is everything, and the mystic who asserts that it is nothing, fail, on this side and on that, to hit the truth. '"Yes, I see, dear; it's about halfway between," Aunt Juley had hazarded in earlier years. No, truth, being alive, was not halfway between anything. It was only to be found by continuous excursions into either realm, and, though proportion is the final secret, to espouse it at the outset is to ensure sterility' (pp. 195–6). Henry is not necessarily opposed to connecting, though he opposes anything interfering with his ability to see life steadily. At first he lacks understanding of the need to connect, later the ability to do so, and Margaret eventually bursts out at him, 'You shall see the connection if it kills you' (p. 300).

'Only connect' is provocatively incomplete. This is re-interpreted by Peter Widdowson: 'Normally read as Forster's positive imperative: "All we must do is connect," it suggests too the plaintive, despairing tones of a fading faith; "If only we could connect"' (1977, p. 12). Ian Milligan hands the phrase to the reader: 'It may well be that the point of the novel lies in challenging the reader to decide what it is proper and profitable to join together' (1987, p. 67). Christopher Gillie is clearer: 'The epigraph is both a judgement and an appeal: a judgement on a society which knows no other ways to understand connections, and an appeal to human imagination and sensitivity to take responsibility for accident so as to transform it into meaning and shape coincidence into coherence' (1983, pp. 123–4).

Connecting is sometimes treated quite lightly. Leonard boasts: 'I'm connected with a leading insurance company' (p. 147). When just after Margaret tries to explain why he has impressed them, he splutters 'I fail to see the connection', Margaret persists: 'We hoped there would be a connection between last Sunday and other days' (p. 148). For Leonard Margaret-and-Helen are connected into a whole: '"The Miss Schlegels" still remained a composite Indian god, whose waving arms and contradictory speeches were the product of a single mind' (p. 146).

The possible connections include that of place (by train or on foot, not by car) of different classes ('We tried knowing another class – impossible', p. 147) and of people, a matter of personal relations, whether of friendship or marriage, between sisters and between men and women.

More abstractly, Forster names two polarities, monk/beast and prose/passion. Many more can be found, overlapping and of varying degrees of precision: Culture/Business, England/Germany, heart/head, seen/unseen, city/country, past/present, contemplation/action, warp (money)/woof, life/death, seeing steadily/seeing whole. All these are touched on: the need for balance, and the difficulty of achieving it, emerge, in action.

How much connecting is there? The Schlegel sisters connect England and Germany, and may even embody the best of both. Margaret and Helen fully connect with each other. Marriage provides a strained connection between Schlegels and Wilcoxes. The child of Schlegel and Bast inherits, and plays – across class divisions – with young Tom. The most profound connection, though, is Margaret with Mrs Wilcox, the live woman and the dead, and with the house, representing as it does beauty, tradition and the country.

'Only connect' is deliberately vague, and working out the meaning (and then how actually to bring about connection) is left to the reader.

iii   Value Culture

Thirty years after *Howards End*, Forster wrote a short essay with an ambitious title, 'Does Culture Matter?', and a casual tone:

> Culture is a forbidding word. I have to use it, knowing of none better, to describe the various beautiful and interesting objects which men have made in the past, and handed down to us, and which some of us are hoping to hand on ... We have, in this age of unrest, to ferry much old stuff across the river, and the old stuff is not merely books, pictures and music, but the power to enjoy and understand them ... Cultivated people are a drop of ink in the ocean ... Culture, thank goodness, is no longer a social asset, it can no longer be employed either as a barrier against the mob or as a ladder into the aristocracy ... What we have got is (roughly speaking) a little knowledge about books, pictures, tunes, runes, and a little skill in their interpretation ... We inherit a tradition which has lasted for about three thousand years ... People today are either indifferent to the aesthetic products of the past (that is the position both of the industrial magnate and of the trade unionist) or else (the Communist position) they are suspicious of them ... Our chief job is to enjoy ourselves and not to lose heart, and to spread culture not because we love our fellow men, but because certain things seem to us unique and priceless, and, as it were, push us out into the world on their service.   (*Two Cheers for Democracy*, 1965, pp. 108–14)

Forster's approach here suggests more complete confidence in the value of traditional culture than any post-Victorian can achieve. Trilling remarks that Forster is 'perhaps unique among modern novelists' in 'his understanding of the part played by art in the life of the middle classes' (1944, p. 47) – in fact in the life of a small section of the middle class resembling the Schlegels.

This topic in the novel is introduced by Aunt Juley, who asks Margaret: 'Do [the Wilcoxes] care about Literature and Art? That is most important when you come to think of it. Literature and Art. Most important' (p. 23). The Schlegels would not phrase it thus directly, perhaps not even make it so central. They do, however, connect with Wilcoxes at a cathedral and with Leonard Bast at a concert (and later fail to connect with him in another cathedral). They hear Beethoven's Fifth practically every time it is played in London (p. 123), and know of Monet and Debussy. Otherwise, the references are to lesser artists where the tone suggests questioning of their culture. Margaret surprisingly cannot tell Cruikshanks from Gillrays (p. 167), unless this is explained by the tension of awaiting Henry's proposal. At the lunch party for Mrs Wilcox, Margaret is 'placing Rothenstein' (p. 84), 'zigzagging with her friends over Thought and Art' (p. 86). 'Clever talk' is dismissed as 'the social counterpart of a motor-car, all jerks' (p. 84) – and Forster despises cars.

He appears to expect his readers to have associations for Monet and Debussy, to be able to pronounce *Tannhauser* correctly, to be able to afford the price of a ticket to a Queen's Hall concert – and to own umbrellas. The circle perhaps is smaller: an elite who fully appreciate even a minor contemporary painter like William Rothenstein, rather than merely glibly 'place' him. Perhaps Forster mocks both groups, asserting the wisdom of those who do not follow current fashions, who do not 'keep up with Wedekind or John' (p. 258).

Forster's point may be the inability to value Brahms above MacDowell, or a critique of a superficial approach to culture – zigzagging over thought and art resembles T. S. Eliot's criticism in 'The Love Song of J. Alfred Prufrock': 'Across the room the women come and go / Talking of Michelangelo'. The issue may be of talking – part of Margaret's learning during the novel is the advance from talking too much, leading 'the lives of gibbering monkeys' (p. 88; we now speak of 'the chattering classes') to silence. The Schlegels consume culture, but write only letters and are not seen painting or playing the piano (unlike Lucy of *A Room with a View*, who expresses herself through music before she is able to do so in life).

'In Britain today we all want to be Schlegels', wrote Noel Annan in 1977 ('The Path to British Decadence', *Sunday Times*, 22 May 1977,

p. 34). In the Thatcherite eighties, we all wanted to be Wilcoxes and be rich instead.

Leonard also cares about 'Literature and Art', as a means to 'improving' himself and 'getting a wider outlook' (p. 65). His culture is a Queen's Hall concert, seeing three operas at Covent Garden in less than year, and some nineteenth century books. His culture, indeed, may be more timeless than the Schlegels' pursuit of what's new. Leonard attempts to connect John Ruskin's prose to himself: 'Was there anything to be learned from this fine sentence? Could he adapt it to the needs of daily life?' (p. 62).

Leonard – and Forster – think only of High Culture. Other forms of culture are rarely suggested. Jacky sings a chorus of a music-hall song (p. 64). Carols in Westminster Abbey on Christmas Day are a communal ritual (p. 91), as is Mrs Wilcox's funeral for the Hilton villagers: 'The funeral of a rich person was to them what the funeral of Alcestis or Ophelia is to the educated. It was Art; though remote from life, it enhanced life's values' (p. 98). Forster, it seems, could not share T. S. Eliot's enjoyment of Marie Lloyd, knew nothing of folk songs, or of the strengths George Orwell found in working-class culture, which he presented as a world of whippets, pigeon-racing and knowledgeability about soccer.

Mrs Wilcox has a culture of a wholly different kind, valuing an old house, the vine, the wych-elm, 'the paddock that she loved more dearly than the garden itself', (p. 102), wild flowers, and the folklore past of pig's teeth pushed into a tree trunk.

Culture requires leisure, available to few. Too easily it becomes a matter of keeping up with, of placing, or of something to talk about. Culture can be inhuman: Tibby finds Oxford beautiful but makes no friends (pp. 113–14): his role is to show that being 'profoundly versed in counterpoint' (pp. 44–5) need not lead to sweetness and light. That much of the culture is of the past (Beethoven and Brahms come together with Gillray and Ricketts here) connects the Schlegels to Mrs Wilcox.

Forster only gently and obliquely questions Culture, but prompts the reader (a Schlegel: the Wilcoxes do not read novels like Forster's) to ask what this really means. Is it about going to concerts and art galleries? Given dependence on money and education, are there ways to make it more accessible? Is the point of it all to zigzag across Thought and Art, to compare Monet and

Debussy cleverly? Or is Culture a means to achieving an inner life and a proper valuing of the unseen?

iv   Value Nature

Responding to Nature transcends both Culture and Business in the novel. Nature offers beauty, stability, the seasonal cycle. Forster is easy to follow here, but his pastoral is written when this strain is well-established in literature and he has little or nothing to add. The country of course is superior to the city. Forster wrote later in *Abinger Pageant*: 'Houses and bungalows, hotels, restaurants and flats, arterial roads, by-passes, petrol pumps and pylons – are these going to be England? Are these man's final triumph? Or is there another England, green and eternal, which will outlast them? . . . You can make a town, you can make a desert, you can even make a garden; but you can never, never make the country, because it was made by Time' ('The Abinger Pageant', *Abinger Harvest*, 1936, p. 363).

Broadly, Forster is within the Romantic convention which can be dated as beginning in 1765 when Rousseau, on his island in the Lake of Bienne, listened to the waves until he became completely at one with Nature – a view of the world which found its full expression in Britain in Wordsworth and Constable. Roger Ebbatson suggests: 'In his concern for humane values, in his stress upon individual response, and in his criticism of conformity both social and religious, Forster stands as the heir to Romanticism. To his omnipresent themes of sincerity, freedom and culture should be added one which comes to assume crucial significance: the primacy of Nature, and man's organic connexion with the natural world . . . *The Longest Journey, Howards End* and *Maurice* all finally endorse the supremacy of Nature, and the genuine human life as one organically connected with Nature' (1980, pp. 210, 211). Judith Weissman presents *Howards End* as 'the last great English novel of Romantic radicalism' (1987, p. 262).

Thinking and writing about Nature, however, kept finding new directions in the nineteenth century. W. J. Keith suggests 'the occurrence, sometime in the 1880s, of an urban-rural dissociation of sensibility' (1974, p. 150). Though this may be a late date, Forster's childhood conveniently fits. Keith documents the writers who, with firsthand experience, shaped Forster's response to the countryside: W. H. Hudson, Edward Thomas, H. J. Massingham,

who wrote: 'In our depths we are a country, not an urban people.'
These writers – and specifically Richard Jefferies, George Borrow,
R. L. Stevenson and E. V. Lucas – inspire Leonard's adventure, the
night walk in the Surrey woods.

Forster may be placed not at the tail-end of the Romantic view
of Nature but as anticipating Georgian Poetry, the poems collected
by Edward Marsh in five anthologies between 1912 and 1922 and
featuring such poets as Rupert Brooke and W. H. Davies. The
point was made by C. K. Stead in 1964: 'The Georgians belonged
to the new intellectual group that grew steadily in numbers during
the first decade of this century; and their type is perhaps best
illustrated by the Schlegel sisters in E. M. Forster's novel *Howards
End*' (p. 85). Kim A. Herzinger picks up the point, asserting that
Howards End is 'the best and the most typical twentieth-century
novel to be thoroughly cast in the Georgian mold . . . *Howards End*
may serve as a happy introduction to certain themes and issues that
preoccupied all of the Georgians. The most important of these
themes and issues is man's relationship with nature; for Forster,
as for the Georgians, the rural or organic image provides "almost
the essential alternative myth for the era, the only outright model
of community as opposed to crowd"' (1982, pp. 68–9).

Margaret's role at the women's debate is to be the advocate for
'the Society for the Preservation of Places of Historic Interest or
Natural Beauty' (p. 133) – precisely her role as countrywoman
presiding finally at Howards End.

While the love of Nature is a familiar theme to which Forster
could not add much, his faith in the farmworker is a rather
different note, beginning with Leonard's observations walking out
of the village of Hilton, and soon shifting to the narrator's hopes:
'Hilton was asleep, or, at the earliest, breakfasting. Leonard noticed
the contrast when he stepped out of it into the country. Here men
had been up since dawn. Their hours were ruled, not by a London
office, but by the movements of the crops and the sun. That they
were men of the finest type only the sentimentalist can declare. But
they kept to the life of daylight. They are England's hope. Clumsily
they carry forward the torch of the sun, until such time as the nation
sees fit to take it up. Half clodhopper, half board-school prig, they
can still throw back to a nobler stock, and breed yeomen' (p. 314).
Accepting this as Leonard's observation, he cannot be expected to
have much insight into the actual lives of these 'yeomen'. Henry

sees truly – for once – when he says 'The days for small farms are over . . . Smallholdings, back to the land – ah! Philanthropic bunkum' (p. 205). Lewis Grassic Gibbon, writing in *Sunset Song* of Scots farming from within at this date, had the same insight, 'the day of the crofter was fell near finished' (1932, Pan, 1973, p. 74). Such texts as Arnold Wesker's *Roots* (1959) and Ronald Blythe's *Akenfield* (1969) supply more accurate pictures of life down on the farm. Yet Forster cannot be placed alone in an unconvincing view: 'three acres and a cow' was a late nineteenth century prescription to solve England's problems, and Hilaire Belloc wanted to place other people on 10-acre plots when Forster was writing. English affection for country life after all continues: *The Archers* has lasted forty years on BBC radio and 'Country Diary' remains one of the most popular features in *The Guardian*. Forster, writing of Miss Avery's farm, comments that 'the country, which we visit at weekends, was really a home to it' (p. 264) and in fact the rural cottage as weekend retreat is far more popular (and dreamed of) today than in 1910.

The country and the people who live and work in it are good; the city and suburbia are both something between evil and merely dubious. The big city can, after all, offer Beethoven in Queen's Hall; the smaller city can be as beautiful as Oxford. If only the city could be as natural as a river and as unchanging as Howards End! Yet mobility and rootlessness are inevitable in the city, and the car becomes symbolic of this, stinking, raising dust, killing a cat at Oniton and colliding with a horse and cart near Ripon in Yorkshire (p. 96).

v Some Other Ideas

The attitude to business is finally mixed. Margaret says decisively that the world's work needs to be done (p. 177). This led D. H. Lawrence to denounce Forster in a letter: 'You did make a nearly deadly mistake glorifying those business people in *Howards End*. Business is no good' (*The Letters of D. H. Lawrence*, IV, ed. Warren Roberts, James T. Boulton and Elizabeth Mansfield, Cambridge University Press, 1987, p. 301). Yet Forster sees it as essential to civilise the business mind, which in the novel may fail with Henry and almost certainly fails with Charles and Paul. So if the humanising fails, is the only alternative to break the business man – and is imprisoning his son the only way to do this?!

Two of Bernard Shaw's major plays of the period have other answers. In *Major Barbara* the Professor of Greek will succeed the capitalist, but Shaw does not show whether Cusins comes to accept the capitalists' methods, or is able to transform them. In *Heartbreak House* Hesione is able to fascinate Boss Mangan and her strange house prompts him to odd behaviour: he starts to strip. Shaw's final answer, though, is to eliminate him, with a bomb in the gravel pit. The same play also diagnoses the decline of England and the cause of the First World War as due to the ruling class abdicating its responsibilities in the frivolity and idleness of Hesione, Hector, and Ariadne, and the ineffectual idealism of Mazzini Dunn.

The world of Culture is, in the 1990s, constantly expected to connect with Business. So the Royal Shakespeare Company is 'saved' from deeper debt by the Royal Insurance Company and the English Shakespeare Company depends on the Allied Irish Bank. Sport receives eight times as much corporate support as culture. What the artists find is that business is interested first in the bottom line, and then in the conventional and unchallenging. Has the business mind, one wonders, changed since Forster created Henry?

Forster's mistrust of Business and praise of Culture and Nature make him one of the many writers Martin Wiener blames for British industrial decline. The nation depended on industry, but society chose instead to feel superior to trade, commerce and factories. Bruce Page comments that the two worlds were not only opposed, but that there was also a sense that one mattered more: 'Our most dangerous inheritance from the Victorians, as Martin Wiener shows us, is the belief that culture and technology, or literature and science, city and countryside (finally, one suspects, body and mind) are separate principles of existence, opposed to each other on the implicit proposition that one is superior in human affairs, and the other is inferior' (1981, p. 19). Anthony Sampson has an answer:

The obvious solution might seem to be to respect both sets of values: to give incentives and respect to the industrialists and technologists who are essential for Britain's survival, while giving dignity, opportunity or poetry to those people who are not. But the conflict of values, as Professor Wiener's book reminds us, is never easy to resolve. English history in the Eighties, he believes, may turn on 'a cultural contest between the two faces of the middle class'. Looking at the implications of both, I can only hope that they both win.   (1981, p. 11)

In two words, only connect!
Howards End demands a valuing of tradition, the past, less a feudal society than William Morris's dream of a harmonious society. The past had stability, lacking a craze for movement, so the present can learn from this. Forster's attack is on change for change's sake, for fashion's sake (Howards End could not be improved by being rebuilt further from the road, with shrubberies, p. 200), or for profit. Let ancestors help, writes Forster (p. 36).

Extracting other ideas reduces Forster's thought to moralistic tags. Forster urges avoiding excessive faith in talk; trying to see life both steadily and whole; struggling against the daily gray of life. Hope can be found this side of the grave: one of the most important but wistful hopes is that the future of England can be of harmony between classes.

The great strength of *Howards End* may be that its messages are always elusive, not so much criticised elsewhere in the novel as cut down from being absolutes.

Culture and civilisation are shown as superior to businessmen.

Yes, but that's not exactly the conclusion.

True culture feeds the imagination and the inner life, and is not based in the book or the concert-hall.

Yes, but that's not exactly it.

True culture goes hand in hand with personal relations.

Yes, but that's not exactly it.

Cultivating personal relations can lead to sloppiness and let you down, indeed prevent you seeing the world steadily.

Yes, so what else is there?

Beethoven, who knows, remains, and the countryside of England.

Yes, but that's not exactly it.

This leaves the house, the wych-elm, Mrs Wilcox (and a vine, a meadow and Six Hills), which are rich though imprecise symbols – and hope despite reason.

References

Primary

Howards End, ed. Oliver Stallybrass (1910; Abinger Edition, 1973; Penguin Modern Classics, 1975).

Abinger Harvest (London, 1936) (includes his essays 'My Wood', 'Notes on the English Character' and 'The Abinger Pageant').

Aspects of the Novel, ed. Oliver Stallybrass (1927; Abinger Edition, 1974; Penguin, 1976).

Marianne Thornton: a Domestic Biography (London, 1956).

Two Cheers for Democracy (1951; Penguin, 1965) (includes his essays 'The Challenge of our Time', 'What I Believe', 'Does Culture Matter?', 'Not Listening to Music' and 'London is a Muddle').

Bibliographies

McDowell, Frederick P. W., *E. M. Forster: an Annotated Bibliography of Writings about Him* (DeKalb: Northern Illinois University Press, 1976).

Summers, Claude J., *E. M. Forster: a Guide to Research* (London: Garland, 1991).

Secondary Sources

[Includes all the sources quoted in my text, and a selection of other books and articles I have found helpful.]

Allen, Walter, '*Howards End*', *New Statesman*, 19 March 1955, p. 407–8.

— , *The English Novel* (London, 1958).

Amur, G. S., 'Hellenistic Heroines and Sexless Angels: Images of Women in Forster's Novels', *Approaches to E. M. Forster*, ed. Vasant A. Shahane (Atlantic Heights, New Jersey, 1981).

Ashby, Margaret, *Forster Country* (Stevenage, 1991).

Barrett, Elizabeth, 'The Advance beyond Daintiness: Voice and Myth in *Howards End*', *E. M. Forster: Centenary Revaluations*, ed.

Judith Scherer Herz and Robert K. Martin (Toronto, 1982), pp. 155–65.

Batchelor, John, *The Edwardian Novelists* (London, 1982).

Beer, J. B., *The Achievement of E. M. Forster* (London, 1962).

Bell, Michael (ed.), *The Context of English Literature, 1900–1930*, 'Introduction' by Bell (London, 1980).

Blamires, Harry, *Twentieth Century English Literature* (London, 1982).

Bloom, Harold (ed.), *E. M. Forster: Modern Critical Interpretations* (New York, 1987) [reprinted essays].

Bradbury, Malcolm, 'E. M. Forster's *Howards End*', *Critical Quarterly*, 4.3, Autumn 1962, pp. 229–41.

— (ed.), *Forster: A Collection of Critical Essays* (Englewood Cliffs, New Jersey, 1966) [reprinted essays].

Brander, Laurence, *Forster: A Critical Study* (London, 1968).

Brown, E. K., *Rhythm in the Novel* (Toronto, 1950).

Cavaliero, Glen, *The Rural Tradition in the English Novel, 1900–1939* (London, 1977).

— , *A Reading of E. M. Forster* (London, 1979).

Churchill, Thomas, 'Place and Personality in *Howards End*', *Critique*, 5, Spring-Summer 1962, pp. 61–73.

Colmer, John, *E. M. Forster: The Personal Voice* (London, 1975).

— , 'The Modern Condition of England Novel', *Coleridge to Catch-22* (London, 1978), pp. 139–61.

Cox, C. B., *The Free Spirit* (Oxford, 1963), pp. 74–102.

Cowley, Malcolm (ed.), 'E. M. Forster', *Writers at Work*, 1st series (New York, 1957), pp. 23–35 [interview with Forster].

Crews, Frederick C., *E. M. Forster: The Perils of Humanism* (Princeton, New Jersey, 1962).

Daleski, H. M., *Unities* (Athens, Georgia, 1985), pp. 111–25.

Das, G. K., and John Beer, eds., *E. M. Forster: A Human Exploration* (London, 1979).

Delany, Paul, '"Islands of Money": Rentier culture in E. M. Forster's *Howards End*', *English Literature in Transition*, 31.3, 1988, pp. 285–96.

Dowling, David, *Bloomsbury Aesthetics and the Novels of Forster and Woolf* (London, 1985).

Eagleton, Mary, and David Pierce, *Attitudes to Class in the English Novel* (London, 1979).

Ebbatson, Roger, *Lawrence and the Nature Tradition* (Hassocks, Sussex, 1980), pp. 209–38.

Feltes, N. N., *Modes of Production of Victorian Novels* (Chicago, 1986), pp. 76–98.

Finkelstein, Bonnie Blumenthal, *Forster's Women: Eternal Differences* (New York, 1975).

Friedman, Alan, 'The Novel', *The Twentieth Century Mind, I: 1900–1918*, (Oxford, 1972), pp. 414–46.

— , 'Forster and Death', *The Modernists*, ed. Lawrence B. Gamache and Ian S. MacNiven (Rutherford, New Jersey, 1987), pp. 103–13.

Furbank, P. N., 'Ger . . . ', *The Listener*, 31 January 1974, p. 153.

— , *E. M. Forster: A Life* (London, 1977, 1978; one-volume ed., Oxford, 1979).

Gardner, Philip (ed.), *E. M. Forster: The Critical Heritage* (London, 1973).

Gibson, Mary Ellis, 'Illegitimate Order: Cosmopolitanism and Liberalism in Forster's *Howards End*', *English Literature in Transition*, 28, 1985, pp. 106–23.

Gill, Richard, *Happy Rural Seat* (New Haven, Conn., 1973) [tradition of country house novels].

Gillen, Francis, '*Howards End* and the Neglected Narrator', *Novel*, 3, Winter 1970, pp. 139–52.

Gillie, Christopher, *A Preface to Forster* (London, 1983).

Godfrey, Denis, *E. M. Forster's Other Kingdom* (Edinburgh, 1968).

Graham, Kenneth, *Indirections of the Novel: James, Conrad and Forster* (Cambridge, 1988).

Gransden, K. W., *E. M. Forster* (Edinburgh, 1962).

Hardy, John Edward, *Man in the Modern Novel* (Seattle, Wash., 1964).

Henke, Suzette A., '*Howards End*: E. M. Forster without Marx or Sartre', *Moderna Sprak*, 80.2, 1986, pp. 116–20.

Herz, Judith Scherer, and Robert K. Martin, eds., *E. M. Forster: Centenary Revaluations* (Toronto, 1982).

— , 'Evaluating E. M. Forster', *English Literature in Transition*, 27, 1984, pp. 246–48.

Herzinger, Kim A., *D. H. Lawrence in his Time: 1908–1915* (London, 1982), pp. 66–71.

Hoffman, Frederick J., *The Mortal No* (Princeton, New Jersey, 1964).

Howarth, Herbert, 'E. M. Forster and the Contrite Establishment', *Journal of General Education*, 17, 1964, pp. 196–206.

Hoy, Cyrus, 'Forster's Metaphysical Novel', *PMLA*, 75, 1960, pp. 126–36.

Hoy, Pat C., II, 'The Narrow, Rich Staircase in Forster's *Howards End*', *Twentieth Century Literature*, 31, 2–3, Summer–Fall 1985, pp. 221–35.

Hunter, Jefferson, *Edwardian Fiction* (Cambridge, Mass., 1982).

Johnstone, J. K., *The Bloomsbury Group* (New York, 1954).

Karl, Frederick, and Marvin Magalaner, *A Reader's Guide to Great Twentieth Century English Novels* (New York, 1959), pp. 111–19.

Keating, Peter, *Into Unknown England* (London, 1976).

— , *The Haunted Study* (London, 1989).

Keith, W. J., *The Rural Tradition: A Study of the Non-Fiction Prose Writers of the English Countryside* (Toronto, 1974).

Kelvin, Norman, *E. M. Forster* (Carbondale, Illinois, 1967).

Langbaum, Robert, 'A New Look at E. M. Forster', *The Modern Spirit* (New York, 1970), pp. 127–46.

Leavis, F. R., 'E. M. Forster', *The Common Pursuit* (London, 1952), pp. 261–77.

Macaulay, Rose, *The Writings of E. M. Forster* (London, 1938).

Mansfield, Katherine, *Journals*, ed. J. Middleton Murry (London, 1954).

Martin, John Sayre, *E. M. Forster: The Endless Journey* (Cambridge, 1976).

Maskell, Duke, 'Style and Symbolism in *Howards End*', *Essays in Criticism*, 19, July 1969, pp. 292–308 [wholly hostile].

May, Keith M., *Characters of Women in Narrative Literature* (London, 1981).

McConkey, James, *The Novels of E. M. Forster* (Ithaca, N.Y., 1957).

McDowell, Frederick P. W., '"The Mild, Intellectual Light": Idea and Theme in *Howards End*', *PMLA*, 74, 1959, pp. 453–63.

— , *E. M. Forster* (Boston: Twayne, 1969; revised ed., 1982).

— , '"Fresh Woods, and Pastures New": Forster Criticism and Scholarship since 1975', *E. M. Forster: Centenary Revaluations*, ed. Judith Scherer Herz and Robert K. Martin (Toronto, 1982), pp. 311–29.

Messenger, Nigel, *How to Study an E. M. Forster Novel* (London, 1991)

Milligan, Ian, *Howards End* (London: Macmillan Master Guides, 1987).

Moore, G. E., *Principia Ethica* (Cambridge, 1903).

Oliver, H. J., *The Art of E. M. Forster* (Melbourne, 1960).

Page, Bruce, 'Poetry in the Engine-Room', *New Statesman*, 17 April 1981, pp. 18–19.

Page, Norman, *E. M. Forster* (London, 1987).

Parkinson, R. N., 'The Inheritors; or A Single Ticket for *Howards End*', *E. M. Forster: A Human Exploration*, ed. G. K. Das and John Beer (London, 1979), pp. 55–68.

Pinkerton, Mary, 'Ambiguous Connections: Leonard Bast's Role in *Howards End*', *Twentieth Century Literature*, 31, 2–3, Summer-Fall 1985, pp. 236–46 [based on manuscript study].

Priestley, J. B., *The Edwardians* (London, 1970).

Raban, Jonathan, *The Technique of Modern Fiction* (London, 1968).

Rahman, Tariq, 'The Use of the Millenarian Myth in E. M. Forster's *Howards End*', *Studies in English Literature* (Tokyo), 1987, pp. 33–60.

Raskin, Jonah, *The Mythology of Imperialism* (New York, 1971).

Rivenberg, Paul R., 'The Role of the Essayist-Commentator in *Howards End*', *E. M. Forster: Centenary Revaluations*, ed. Judith Scherer Herz and Robert K. Martin (Toronto, 1982), pp. 167–76.

Roby, Kinley E., 'Irony and the Narrative Voice in *Howards End*', *Journal of Narrative Technique*, 2, May 1972, pp. 116–24.

Rockwell, Joan, *Fact into Fiction* (London, 1974).

Rosecrance, Barbara, *Forster's Narrative Vision* (Ithaca, N.Y., 1982).

Russell, John, *Style in Modern British Fiction* (Baltimore, 1978) [technical approach].

Sampson, Anthony, 'When the work ethic has no work', *The Observer*, 7 June 1981, p. 11.

Savage, D. S., *The Withered Branch* (London, 1950).

Schwarz, Daniel R., *The Transformation of the English Novel, 1890–1930* (London, 1989), pp. 116–29.

Scott, P. J. M., *E. M. Forster: Our Permanent Contemporary* (London, 1984).

Shahane, Vasant A. (ed.), *Approaches to E. M. Forster* (Atlantic Heights, New Jersey, 1981).

Shusterman, David, *The Quest for Certitude in E. M. Forster's Fiction* (Bloomington, Indiana, 1965).

Stallybrass, Oliver (ed.), *The Manuscripts of 'Howards End'* (London, 1973).

—, 'Editing Forster', *Essays in Criticism*, 26, October 1976, pp. 373–6.

Stape, John H., 'Editing Forster', *Essays in Criticism*, 26, April 1976, pp. 177–81.

—, 'Leonard's "Fatal Forgotten Umbrella": Sex and the Manuscript Revisions to *Howards End*', *Journal of Modern Literature*, 9.1, 1981–82, 123–32.

Stead, C. K., *The New Poetic* (London, 1964).

Stone, Wilfred, *The Cave and the Mountain: A Study of E. M. Forster* (Stanford, Calif., 1966).

Stubbs, Patricia, *Women and Fiction* (Hassocks, Sussex, 1979).

Summers, Claude J., *E. M. Forster* (New York, 1983).

Thickstun, William R., *Visionary Closure in the Modern Novel* (London, 1988), pp. 30–51.

Thomson, Douglass H., 'From Words to Things: Margaret's Progress in *Howards End*', *Studies in the Novel*, 15.2, Summer 1983, pp. 122–34.

Thomson, George H., *The Fiction of E. M. Forster* (Detroit, 1967).

Tindall, Gillian, *Countries of the Mind: The Meaning of Place to Writers* (London, 1991).

Tindall, William York, *Forces in Modern British Literature, 1885–1956* (New York, 1956).

Trilling, Lionel, *E. M. Forster* (New York, 1943; London, 1944).

VanDe Vyvere, J. L., 'The Mediatorial Voice of the Narrator in E. M. Forster's *Howards End*', *Journal of Narrative Technique*, 6, 1976, pp. 204–15.

Watts, Cedric, *Literature and Money* (Hemel Hempstead, 1990).

Weatherhead, Andrea K., '*Howards End*: Beethoven's Fifth', *Twentieth Century Literature*, 31, 2–3, Summer-Fall 1985, pp. 247–64.

Weissman, Judith, *Half Savage and Hardy and Free: Women and Rural Radicalism in the Nineteenth-Century Novel* (Middletown, Conn., 1987), pp. 262–90.

Westburg, Barry R., 'Forster's Fifth Symphony: Another Aspect of *Howards End*', *Modern Fiction Studies*, 10, Winter 1964–65, pp. 359–65.

Widdowson, Peter, *E. M. Forster's 'Howards End': Fiction as History* (Sussex, 1977).

Wiener, Martin J., *English Culture and the Decline of the Industrial Spirit, 1850–1980* (Cambridge, 1981).

Wilde, Alan, *Art and Order: A Study of E. M. Forster* (New York, 1964).

— (ed.), *Critical Essays on E. M. Forster* (Boston, 1985) [reprinted essays].

Williams, Raymond, *The Country and the City* (London, 1973).

Woolf, Virginia, 'Mr Bennett and Mrs Brown', 1924, *The Captain's Death Bed and other Essays* (New York, 1950).

—, 'The Novels of E. M. Forster', *Collected Essays*, I (London, 1966).

Wright, Andrew, *Fictional Discourse and Historical Space* (London, 1987).

Wright, Anne, *Literature of Crisis, 1910–22* (London, 1984), pp. 23–62.

Index